Simon & Schuster

New York   London   Toronto   Sydney   Tokyo   Singapore

WAYNE A. MYERS, M.D.

Shrink Dreams

Tales from the Hidden Side of Psychiatry

SIMON & SCHUSTER
Simon & Schuster Building
Rockefeller Center
1230 Avenue of the Americas
New York, New York 10020

Designed by Karolina Harris
Manufactured in the United States of America

1   3   5   7   9   10   8   6   4   2

Library of Congress Cataloging-in-Publication Data

Myers, Wayne A.
Shrink dreams: tales from the hidden side of psychiatry/
Wayne A. Myers.
p.   cm.
1. Countertransference (psychology)—Case studies.   I.   Title.
RC489.C68M94   1992
616.89'14—dc20   91-46943
                                                            CIP

ISBN: 0-671-73898-4

To my wife, Joanne,
whose love and loving I dearly cherish,
and to my children, Tracy and Blake,
whom I dearly love.

CONTENTS

INTRODUCTION

I have always hated the word "shrink." Its implications of diminishment, reduction, the wizened head displayed as a trophy by some primitive tribe hardly speaks of expansion, self-fulfillment, the spreading of wings that is the goal of psychotherapy. Yet the word expresses a crucial truth—for the psychotherapist, not for the patient. For it is central to most schools of psychotherapy that the therapist must indeed "shrink" much of that aspect of the outward self that returns a confidence with a confidence and allows the free expression of thoughts and fantasies. The therapist conceals behind an impervious mask his or her private life, who he or she really is. Like the moon, the therapist reflects back so far as possible the glow of a patient's expectations of other people. Thus an imbalance is created in the strange dialogue between two people that is psychotherapy: patients who tell everything about themselves—or as much as they can—and psychotherapists who tell nothing—or so little as to give the merest hint of the whole person, a hint that is as likely to be wrong as right. As a result the common image of psychotherapy is of the vulnerable patient in a chair or on a couch presided over by the great stone face that is the therapist.

Yet, however accepted and necessary to therapy this image may be, questions still simmer in the minds of patients as well as in the general public. What goes on behind that impassive face? What of the therapist's fantasies? Are they simply the corollaries of the patient's wishes for love and death, for sex and submission, inactive for the minutes of the therapy hour? What are we, sitting silently in our leather chairs behind a man or a woman stretched out on a sofa, really thinking about? What are we really like? Are we more daring than our patients? Or more banal? And more to the point, how do our fantasies connect—even interlock—with those of our patients? Do our thoughts, secret wishes, and prejudices affect a patient's progress? And if so, how? For good or ill? What, finally, does a shrink dream?

These are questions often asked by those who seek to understand therapists, those psychological savants who profess to be able to unravel the motives behind the behavior of their patients. And they are questions asked, both covertly and overtly, by patients themselves. Indeed, the very blankness of the therapist can set the patient off on a quest for information about the identity of this person who seems so knowledgeable about his mental life, who even claims to have the power to change it. This quest is, of course, the stuff of therapy. The patient fixes on small clues—a new painting or a photograph on the office wall, a slight change of emphasis in the therapist's voice, which then mix with arcane memories and hidden desires to form a perception of the therapist—a perception based, in large part, on the experiences and dramatis personae from the patient's own life. These perceptions and the reactions to them, which may provide fertile ground for understanding a patient's past, are what we call *transference*.

Transferences occur in settings other than the therapeutic hour. Any one of us—patient or therapist—might, for example, endow our teachers, bosses, and lovers with the feelings and judgments we have linked in the past with our parents. But when, in some belated attempt to master earlier experiences, we begin to behave toward the cast of characters in our current lives in ways that repeat past interactions, we are frequently headed for trouble. In the therapeutic setting, further potential for trouble lies in the fact that behind the great stone face of the therapist there is a mind alive with feelings and desires of its own, feelings and wishes that resonate with the patient's distortions and which the therapist sorts out, according to his or her particular psychotherapeutic approach, in order to help the patient. The feelings summoned up in the therapist by the patient are called *countertransference.*

The feelings aroused during and after a session with a patient may, of course, be appropriate to the particular situation. But they can also be dramatically out of sync with its reality. If we like or dislike a patient, it may simply be a function of that person's being nice or not so nice. But if we feel love or hate for them, we are very probably responding to them as we have to others who were important to us in our own past. Recognizing that, we can guard against such inappropriate—and potentially destructive—feelings. We are, after all, engaged in a uniquely human process in which professional training allows us to use the essence of ourselves to help others toward self-understanding and self-fulfillment.

When a patient tells a therapist that he or she is handsome or beautiful, sexy, smart, or sensuous, any therapist—whether short, plump, and aging or young, naive, and brash—is likely to feel inwardly very pleased and even occasionally to find that siren song irresistible. But again, it's basic to good therapy that we recognize such statements as the result of overheated feelings released as therapy takes hold and that we must defend ourselves against their seductive appeal. If we cannot stop ourselves from responding, we must face the consequences of the tension between our own reactivated needs, wishes, and dreams and those of our patients.

We have all heard stories of the shrink who uses a patient to enact his or her own sexual needs. But there are other ways as well in which therapists can let their countertransference feelings run amok. One may impose on a patient a scenario of revenge for some grievous wrong inflicted in the therapist's early life. Or one may try to rescue a patient from what appears to be a disastrous life situation in order to rewrite the history of some unfortunate person in the therapist's own life. As innocent and well intentioned as some of these enactments may appear to be at first glance, they rarely stand up to any deeper scrutiny because they invariably place the therapist's needs before those of the patient.

A psychotherapist may, on the other hand, avoid enacting his or her countertransference feelings by a detachment so deep that the patient feels abandoned. Equally unacceptable is the therapist who exudes sympathy from every pore or offers his or her own wounds up to the patient as an emblem of their idyllic attachment. Rather, the balanced therapist must be forever open to rethink old personal problems and old personal resolutions, no matter how often they have been worked through before. He must continually analyze himself in relation to his patient and respond appropriately. Only in this way can we be available to allow a patient to seek and find the solution to a problem that is uniquely his.

Therapists must not allow themselves the comfort of believing that they have ever fully resolved the problems in their own lives. At least nine or ten times a day, they must open themselves to reexperience their old pains, to walk the high-voltage wires of their own childhood trauma, as memories and feelings are aroused during the treatment hours with their patients. And however exhilarating this capacity for openness may be, it is wrenching and exhausting. Sometimes we want a rest, a vacation from the intensity of the therapy hours. And sometimes we allow our own dreams and needs to take over and command center stage, thus inviting problems for our patients and ourselves.

While it is perfectly natural for a therapist to feel a variety of emotions in respect to a patient, to act upon one's own dreams and fantasies as they well up is entirely inappropriate. Envy, love, revenge, sexual desire, and a longing for a sense of meaning in one's life are powerful motivating factors. Yet every therapist I've ever known, treated, or supervised in my more than thirty years in the field of psychiatry has experienced most of these feelings and a host of other emotional juggernauts in their interactions with their patients. Most therapists manage to contain these powerful feelings within acceptable bounds and to keep their countertransference slip ups within the realm of minor misfirings. A few, however, enact their needs and dreams with their patients in so dramatic a fashion as to tarnish the overall reputation of our profession. How, then, can we therapists avoid letting our own needs run roughshod over those of our patients?

The only reasonable answer to this question is for therapists to undergo their own personal therapy before we allow them the license to inflict their unresolved feelings on their patients. Thirty years ago, nearly everyone involved in the mental health professions underwent extensive personal treatment, either psychoanalysis proper or at the very least an analytically oriented form of psychotherapy, along with their training. Today this is the exception rather than the rule. It is particularly true in most of the psychiatric residency training programs in our nation, where the guiding philosophy seems to be one of steering the budding psychiatrist toward a familiarity with the neurobiologic and the psychopharmacologic rather than with the psychodynamic and the interpersonal.

In saying this, I am not advocating a return to the dark days and darker treatments that antedated the golden age of psychotropic medications in which we are now living. I am a firm believer in the use of such drugs when they are called for. Rather, I am saying that therapists must not be trained to practice by the prescription pad alone. Nor should they specialize solely in neurobiologic research, no matter how valuable this may prove to be for generations of patients yet unborn, unless they plan to limit the extent of their careers to the environs of their laboratories.

If at some time during the course of their working lives, these therapists plan to become involved in the treatment of patients and have only received minimal training in the basic workings of the unconscious mind or in the art and science of psychotherapy, then at the very least they will become confused when they begin to work with these patients. If we add to this the fundamental lack of information these therapists have about their own unconscious emotional blocks, as a result of not having received any therapy of their own, the groundwork is inevitably laid for the twin problems of confusion about the process of psychotherapy itself and an inability to deal with the dangerous blind spots of countertransference.

This book embraces a wide variety of cases where the dreams of a therapist take precedence over those of a patient —for good or ill. These cases are the exceptions rather than the rule in most psychotherapies and are not meant to discredit the vast majority of conscientious, caring psychotherapists whose diligent work daily comforts and enhances the lives of those whom they treat. Yet some therapists do create problems, and that is why I have chosen to focus on this particular group. In one instance, I describe how my own unresolved countertransference problems at an earlier period in my career directly interfered with my treatment of a particular patient. The other cases draw upon myriad supervisions which I have conducted with social workers, psychologists, psychiatric residents, graduate psychiatrists, and psychoanalytic candidates over the past thirty years. I have also drawn on the dreams and wishes expressed by the countless therapists whom I have treated, sat with at conferences and meetings, spoken to and read about during these past three decades. For the sake of confidentiality, I have had to change such details as names, locations, professions, and other minor circumstantial and identifying details in the cases I describe. But all of these are actual cases, and I have attempted to preserve faithfully the nature of the specific issues and interactions which arose and then were recognized and in some cases resolved.

Since most of the material for this book derives from my experience as a supervisor of psychotherapists, a few words about the field of supervision seem in order. In psychotherapy training programs in the past, one method of imparting infor-

INTRODUCTION

mation about the course and treatment of specific mental illnesses was through didactic lectures. Another, and generally more popular, vehicle involved a type of on-the-job-training whereby an experienced therapist supervised the budding trainee in his or her work with a patient. When these twin training techniques were coupled with the trainee's own personal analysis, the foundation for learning good therapeutic technique was laid.

In doing supervision, the experienced therapist is often placed in an ambiguous position. The job calls for a perfect amalgam of the roles of educator and therapist. Interventions by the supervisor generally focus on the understanding of specific material brought up by the patient or of specific interventions made by the supervisee. Most often these comments by the supervisor are intended to be educational in nature, as in a discussion of how best to frame a particular question or to time a particular interpretation with a patient. Occasionally, however, the supervisor is faced with the dilemma of just whose psychopathology to focus on most directly, that of the patient being treated or that of the therapist (supervisee) who is treating him.

If we simply point out the presence of a countertransference blind spot to our supervisees, so that they may deal with it in their own treatment, we are clearly staying within the bounds of accepted supervisory practices. If we attempt to analyze directly the meaning of such a block with the supervisee, we have surrendered our educational function and taken on the role of therapist. This may be unavoidable, as when the person we are supervising is not (or has never been) in treatment and is unwilling to submit to this avenue of enlightenment.

Some examples of a therapist's countertransference blind spots are so dramatic as to defy belief, as in "The Dream of Sexual Possession," in which a therapist's ambiguity about his own sexual identity became imposed on that of his patient in a way that was shattering to both the patient and the therapist. I was called in to pick up the pieces at a time when my own analysis was incomplete, and I was so deeply conflicted by what I saw and heard that my effectiveness in dealing with my supervisee, Larry, was limited. I believe that would be different now, although my shock and anger at abuses in the name of therapy have not changed.

Alicia's story was quite different. This beautiful young woman, whose work with me is described in "The Dream of Revenge," yearned to make her long-dead mother suffer. This murderous wish, which had eluded any effective resolution in her previous therapy, threatened to destroy her treatment of an older woman whose resemblance to her mother was more than Alicia could bear.

For over twenty-five years, I have been deeply involved in the field of interracial treatments and supervisions. As a result, I have become familiar with many of the fantasies which members of different races harbor about each other. The specific expressions which these fantasies take, however, can be difficult to penetrate. In the case of Joyce, a black therapist, I uncovered a wish-induced countertransference which distorted her handling of a young white patient who came to her for treatment. Only the recollection of certain specific revelations from her own tragic past, as described in "The Dream of Being White," helped Joyce to reassume the therapeutic mantle she was so well trained to wear.

In working with Leonard, I encountered a therapist whose envy of his patient's wealth and power caused him to collude with the man's character defects rather than to analyze them. The short-term gains and long-term losses described in "The Dream of Envy" serve as a cautionary tale. That Leonard's greed paralleled his patient's was a function of the inadequacy of his own psychotherapy.

Under the guise of saving a young woman in jeopardy, Gabriel, the male therapist I write of in "The Dream of Rescuing a Damsel in Distress," attempted to act out a variety of unsavory and unanalyzed feelings of his own at his patient's expense. When he adamantly refused my suggestion to get therapy, I was forced to blur the boundaries of our interaction and to use the supervision to begin to give him the help he needed. It was a role I felt very uncomfortable with then and still do today, because it severely limits the level of my effectiveness in either sphere.

Sometimes, as with Stan in "The Dream of Letting Go," I have come across an immensely inhibited therapist who unconsciously encouraged a promiscuous patient's sexual excesses as a means of gratifying and expressing aspects of a personality cut off from conscious awareness. The only real answer to such a countertransference was further therapy. Similarly with a therapist who felt empty and depressed, a shrink who felt "shrunken" and suffered from ennui hungered for strong stimulus, as Henry did in "The Dream of Overcoming Emptiness in One's Own Life." However, the best cure for the doctor may not be the best cure for the patient, and my work with Henry was ultimately unsuccessful because of his refusal to enter psychotherapy.

Terry had had some treatment of her own. Only it was left incomplete when her therapist died. As a result, her unanalyzed and unrealized needs for motherhood caused her to assume a highly questionable therapeutic approach with a patient she never should have consented to treat in the first place. In the case of "The Dream of Having the Perfect Child," the treatment arena becomes once again the site for redressing the narcissistic slights and grievances of the therapist's own past.

Edie, too, had had an abbreviated therapy of her own, which unfortunately had barely scratched the surface of the reservoir of rage she harbored toward older people, the group she chose to work with. As a result, she was unaware of her sadistic need to devastate their lives under the guise of helping them. The mayhem her misguided therapeutic ardor caused is illustrated in "The Dream of Sadism."

While negative countertransference feelings can lead to bizarre outcomes in therapy, there are also positive effects which may ensue from understanding one's countertransference. In "The Dream of Finding a Good Father," I describe

INTRODUCTION

how my own feelings about my father influenced the course of the treatment I was conducting with an older male patient. What finally made that particular treatment a success was brought about through the help I received from both an empathetic supervisor and a skillful psychoanalyst.

Over the years, I have developed quite a useful stone face of my own, and I believe firmly in its efficacy. Nonetheless, I believe that demystifying the process of psychotherapy clarifies rather than diminishes it. Knowledge acquired by outsiders doesn't detract from the power of the shaman, savant, or priest. But a patient is not an outsider. A patient is a partner in collaboration fueled by pain and the desire for triumph. And in that collaboration, every patient deserves a shrink whose dreams are not ever beyond control.

CHAPTER 1

The Dream of Sexual Possession

I thought I had heard just about every dream there was, until Larry presented me with his dream toward the end of a hot summer in the late 1960s. And even then I was slow to catch on to one of the strangest erotic nightmares I have ever been privy to.

If you heard only Larry's voice, you would imagine a tall, lanky, white-suited and goateed southern colonel. But when you saw the short round body and the puckish face, the brown eyes mocking behind big horn-rimmed glasses, you would think him a compatible fellow you would want to know better. That's how I felt about this young psychiatrist, who had just the previous spring graduated into the world of private practice.

Although he had had some good supervisors during his psychiatric residency, Larry still exuded a feeling of tentativeness, of something unresolved and urgent behind the formal manner and the broad Georgia accent. He had called me after having heard me "perform" well as the guest lecturer at a case conference at the hospital where he had trained. "I'm scared, Wayne," he said on the telephone, "scared shitless. You've got to help me."

"Of course, Larry," I said, assuming he was suffering from the panic that hits most young psychiatrists early in their first year when they realize they're finally flying solo. "What can I do for you?"

He calmed down and with much hesitation began to tell me about some trouble he was having with a patient. I then arranged to meet with him at once for a supervisory session.

But at that first session of private supervision, Larry showed none of the urgency he had expressed over the phone. In a low voice, empty of emotion, his accent all but flattened out, he launched into the case of a young woman whom he had been seeing for some months. Betsy was a tall, blond banker who was struggling to break away from her Social Register family, a family as WASP and waspish as they come. Although she had been away from home during her years in prep school and college and was now living in her own apartment in Manhattan, she could not keep herself from going home every weekend to Connecticut to see her family—and suffering the whole time.

"The way it is, Wayne, is every Sunday night after the visit is over and she gets into her car and sees the pillars of that big transplanted southern mansion receding in the rearview mirror, she tells herself she'll never go back again. But then comes Friday night and she gets in her car and, before she knows it, the Merritt Parkway's unrolling under her once again. And she's trying to hug that ice goddess mother of hers and wrench away the silver cocktail shaker from her father, who's usually put away several martinis by the time she gets there." Larry shivered, as if it was his own mother and his own father he was speaking of.

There was something odd about the way Larry dwelt on the details of Betsy's weekends in Greenwich, the heavy silver cocktail shaker looming rather larger than the young woman herself, as if it was more real to him than she was. There was something very odd about Larry's way of seeing things, I thought. But just how odd, how bizarre and sexually overpowering, I would not learn for quite a while.

My sessions with Larry continued, and most of my early supervisory interventions with him on this case were along educational lines. I would suggest certain articles in the literature that might help him understand aspects of Betsy's problems. I would also comment on his technique of framing questions or interpretations and point out how inappropriate some of the remarks he made to Betsy were. For example, at the fifth session he informed me that he had told Betsy he had been thinking all weekend about whether she had managed not to leave the city that Friday.

"But, Larry," I cut in, "what do you think the primary message in your communication to her was?"

"What do you mean?" he asked, as if he had never heard such a question before.

"What were you *really* telling her?"

"I guess I was trying to show her that I care about what she does, that I want her to get out of that dreadful family scene, that I want her to *change,*" he replied as if the answer should be obvious.

I said nothing, waiting for him to think it through further, which he did.

"You mean I shouldn't have introduced myself into the equation?" he finally asked.

"It's kind of seductive of you to tell her that you've been thinking about her all weekend," I said, then paused to let my comment sink in. "How is she supposed to read that? How does she distinguish between your caring for her as a patient and your caring for her as a woman?"

Larry was silent for some time and I began to think about how little I really knew this man. What kind of woman did he like? Did he have a live-in girlfriend? He had never referred to anyone, only to the sort of southern girls who were the belle of the ball in his youth, so flirtatious and out of reach, swathed in tulle and smelling of gardenias. Maybe behind that courtly manner of his he was more fragile than I realized.

He finally spoke, trying to think the question through. "Do you really believe I'm too seductive with her?"

"A bit," I said. "Maybe it's something you ought to take up in your own therapy."

"That's a problem," he said, hesitating.

"What do you mean?"

"I wasn't too happy with my therapist," he said. "I liked her but she could be pretty judgmental at times, so I left her." His glance at me reminded me of my comments at the case conference where I had met him. I had spoken about judgmentalism and its dangers. He knew it was one of my *bêtes noires*. "Only I'm not absolutely sure," he added. "Could be it wasn't her but me projecting my shit onto her."

Something about that remark bothered me. It felt insincere and evasive, as if Larry was somehow pandering to my beliefs and not expressing his own. He knew I wasn't happy with the idea of judgmental therapists. And he knew I knew he was not either. So why was he beating around the bush? What was really bothering him?

"You know, Larry," I said, "I have the feeling you're skirting around the edges of something now and I'm not sure what or why. I know we're out of time but maybe next week we can get down to something more substantial, something you and I can really sink our teeth into, instead of the white bread you've been feeding me thus far."

He just looked at me, his round face blank, the brown eyes behind his glasses unreadable. Then he got up, nodded goodbye, and left my office.

I wondered just who his therapist was. He had referred to *her,* so I knew he was seeing a woman. But I didn't know her name. That is one of those questions that protocol demands you not push for an answer to from someone in supervision with you. It's fine for the supervisee to volunteer that sort of information, but if you ask and receive no reply, that's as far as you can go. Besides, why did I really want to know her identity? Was it simply my own competitiveness coming out? Or did it have something to do with Larry's reason for leaving her?

I had lots to think about for the next week—or four weeks as it turned out. Larry called to cancel our next three supervisory sessions. I wondered whether I had blown it by being so blunt. But then he kept the fourth appointment and finally dropped the bombshell. As soon as he walked into my office, I knew something was up. He looked thinner, and there was a tightness about his mouth that made me realize he was extremely anxious. "I want to talk about a different patient today, Wayne, if you don't mind," he said, obviously intending to charge ahead whether I minded or not.

"By all means," I answered.

"It's about Darrell, that is, Darlene," he began. "It started last fall when I was the admitting psychiatrist on call at ———," and he named a well-known private psychiatric hospital. "That's where I first met him, er, *her,*" he emphasized, as if having to remind himself of the gender of this patient. It was a confusion he would often continue to fall into as he poured out his tale.

"You were moonlighting?" I asked, knowing that such extracurricular activities are frowned upon at the training hospital to which he was attached.

"Yes," he said. "You know how it is, Wayne, you *need* the money. My family doesn't have much to spare, what with keeping the house up and paying the few servants they still have. And they don't like it that I've come up north to work." He paused. "Daddy had just sent me a letter telling me he couldn't advance me any more money, making me feel so *vacated.*" Then he blurted out, "When Darrell came that night he slipped into my life like the fulfillment of a promise." And Larry stopped and fell into a morose silence.

"Darrell?" I asked, not knowing whether we were talking about Darrell or Darlene.

"Yes. When he walked through the door that night, his kinky black hair glistening from the rain the way sheep's wool does, and the raindrops pouring down his face, he didn't look a bit like anyone I would want," Larry said, his voice shaking, "or ever have anything in common with. But then he began to tell me his story, and even though he was clearly upset, he managed to put it all together clearly from beginning to end— or the end he had reached by coming to see me—which turned out to be a sort of beginning. You see, his life wasn't at all like mine and yet it was. I *knew* him, knew his speech, so soft and lulling even though he'd been born in the North."

It was then I realized that Darrell was a black man. "Yes," Larry went on, "he told me his whole story that night. When I saw how long it was going to take, I told him to wait until my hospital shift was over, and then we went out to a coffee shop and talked until daylight.

"Darrell told me all about himself, from the time he was born. He was the third child of an unwed mother and it was him his mother preferred over his older brother and sister. He was *her* child, her precious baby, and 'Precious' was what she mostly called him." Here Larry sounded the plaintive note of all those children who feel themselves not to have been their mother's favorite. "His father was a passive guy who, so far as I could make out, allowed her to exclude him from having much of anything to do with any of the children, but Darrell was especially protected. He was a beautiful baby at birth and only grew more handsome as the years went on."

"He told you that?"

"His mother told *him* that. He and she had some unspoken bond between them, as though the umbilical cord that had connected them in utero would never be severed. For the first few years of Darrell's life, he said the two of them were like Siamese twins fused at the sternum. Just as my mama's old black nurse was with me. Darrell's mother would carry him in her arms, each pair of eyes mirroring the innermost thoughts and feelings of the other's soul, as though they were a single being. Darrell had no idea that he wasn't a little girl."

Larry looked at me and caught me trying to mask my skepticism. "But this idyll ended, as most do," he went on bitterly, "when he had to go to school. With her adored baby away all day, the mother began to drink. And Darrell hated being away from her all that time, only to come home in the afternoon and find her woozy and *away* from him. And on top of that, school was hell. Feeling himself to be a little girl, he hadn't any idea how to cope with the little boys who teased and mocked him for his feminine ways. He *knew* even way back then he was different."

I had heard or read about similar stories a number of times and I was growing even more skeptical of Larry's unquestioning attitude. But after patiently hearing about Darrell's painful adolescence, experiments with homosexuality while in the army, the death of his mother, and his inevitable suicide attempts, I was finally given the new element I realized I had been waiting for. It was hurled at me with a force that took my breath away.

"When Darrell offered up to me the charred embers of his life," Larry continued, "I felt here was the meaning I'd been seeking for so long, here in that tall, slender body, with its beautiful skin—dead black, both his parents having been Gullahs from South Carolina. He was slim and lean as my father, whom everybody had expected me to take after, until I disappointed everyone and myself and grew up short and pudgy like my dear mama.

"And this beautiful black man in distress was calling on me for help. 'Why can't people see,' he asked me, 'that I'm a woman trapped in a man's body! Why can't they *see* that, Larry? Why?' '*I* see it, Darrell,' I said. And I don't think I'll ever experience so rich and deep a moment as that, the look in his eyes, as though I had opened the door of all doors.

"I'd never known anyone with a story like his, I was never so close to anyone who was so—so *naked,* and he was all mine. There was nowhere else for him to turn. He was a woman trapped in a man's body. I believed that. A butterfly in chrysalis and nobody could see that. At least, nobody until he met me.

"Why can't anyone ever let us be what we want to be?" Larry asked me suddenly, but before I could gather myself together to answer, he dashed on. "Well, I'd had enough of that. When Darrell told me he wanted a sex change, I said to him right then and there, 'I'm going to see to it that you get the operation done somehow! Somewhere! No matter what it takes!'"

True to his word, Larry continued to moonlight and saw Darrell on the sly in an office he borrowed from a friend. For hour after hour, as Larry told the story, he helped Darrell plot out how to deal with the psychiatrists he would encounter in the hospitals Larry would direct him to. Under Larry's tutelage, Darrell learned to do more than scream his desires, instead giving them coherent form and structure. He learned the lingo of hospital, social worker, and psychiatrist that would get him what he wanted. Coached by Larry, he learned a script that played to perfection. The doctors at the medical center he went to approved the choice of surgery. And eventually Darrell was given female hormones and began to develop breasts.

"I didn't go to the hospital from first to last," Larry told me, "but, talking to Darrell every day on the phone, I could imagine the changes that were going on in his body, changes *I* had brought about!"

And Larry looked at me with shining eyes, his round face transfigured, whatever difficulties his achievement had led to forgotten for the moment. "He told me he actually cried the day he pulled bikini underpants over the vagina that had been created surgically for him, and hooked a bra over his new breasts. 'I'm a woman at last,' she told herself, 'and don't have to scream it any more.' For she was now Darlene."

Larry said this simply and quietly as if it was the most natural thing in the world. "I cried later when she told me how, while putting on her makeup at the mirror that morning, she felt as if she had never seen herself clearly before. That was the day she got out of the hospital." He paused, as if reliving that moment so long awaited by both of them.

"We'd agreed I should stay away from the hospital during the period when Darrell was turning into Darlene, because I wanted him, that is, her to emerge full-blown. Ever since I'd heard Darrell's story, I'd been imagining her springing fully formed from my brow." Larry smiled sheepishly at the allusion. It was an image that stayed with me as well, of a glamorous black goddess of wisdom shooting out of the forehead of the fat little Zeus-psychiatrist sitting in the chair across from me. Somehow or other, I knew that Darlene would be glamorous.

"How did you feel all this time?" I asked.

"In suspense. Holding my breath. You know, it's like waiting for a new car to be delivered, and you think that everything will go right in your life when you have all those shiny buttons and gears ready to operate at your beck and call. And it smells so good! As she did when she arrived at my apartment that evening."

My silence must have been almost palpable, for Larry for the first time became defensive.

"Well, where else could we meet? It was a great occasion and I wanted to do something appropriate to it, so I'd asked her to dinner. She'd obviously dabbed herself liberally with the Joy perfume I had sent her as a graduation gift from the hospital. She was also wearing the dress I'd bought her."

Larry pretended not to hear my drawn breath. "She looked smashing in it," he went on, "a bouffant job of pink tulle with a sweetheart neckline like the girls wear at home. When she arrived at my door, I understood for the first time how the sight of someone can really take your breath away. I couldn't speak for a moment. Darlene looked better than I'd dreamed —and my dreams were beauts, as you may imagine.

" 'You're beautiful!' I finally gasped. And I don't think either one of us had dared to think beyond that moment, but it seemed only natural to kiss. And then, as they say in the books, passion took over. I haven't kissed many girls, you know, Wayne, just the wallflowers my mother used to make me go out with, not the belles I was supposed to be longing for but was terrified of. And when my lips touched Darlene's beautiful soft mouth and I felt it giving way, well, it was like nothing I'd ever experienced before. And then I felt my penis rise and she did, too, and just sank into my arms, murmuring, 'Darling, oh darling,' and I was echoing her words back to her.

"The next thing I knew I was fumbling with the zipper on her dress and she was whispering, 'Let me help you, honey,' the endearment as natural as it must once have been on her mother's lips, and then we were in my bed, both of us buck naked, and she was wrapping her long legs around me and pulling me into her, into the vaginal orifice that had been made at my instructions. I thought, She's mine! She's mine! She told me later she felt the most complete sense of joy and union she'd felt since her childhood days with her mother. 'I love you, Larry,' she said over and over, stroking me, 'I love you, I love you, I love you.'

"I could only respond in kind. Here was the woman I'd been looking for all my life. Beautiful and beholden to me and not threatening. Never that. Never would she want me to do something I didn't want to do, or be somebody I didn't want to be. This docile, lovely black woman would never threaten me. And, of course, I never thought of her as a man."

At this point I couldn't help but wonder whether the *True Romances* note Larry was striking meant his feelings were fake, or was it simply the nature of such romantic moments to be banal? He went on to tell me that during the days that followed, the lives of the short white man and the tall, black, newly created woman became inextricably bound. "When we were together, we were able to exclude the world outside, as it had excluded us all our lives. Our bodies and minds felt fused. We were merged into each other forever. At last I had someone of my own, someone neither my mother nor my father could get at.

"And then, about a month ago, everything changed for me," Larry said, looking at me gravely. "I know you may think me some kind of a madman, but I'm not. It happened on the night I'd taken Darlene out to dinner and we'd gone down to one of those Indian restaurants in the East Village where I didn't expect to see anyone who knew me. I wasn't ready yet to present Darlene to the world. And just as the waiter was serving our chicken tikka, a man came in and sat in the far corner of the restaurant who I was sure was *you*."

I started to shake my head but Larry went on. "It didn't

matter whether it *was,* Wayne, and I couldn't really *see* in the dimness of that place, but what mattered was that I *thought* it was you. I sort of gasped and Darlene looked up and asked me if I was feeling well. I guess I'd gone pale or something. But it was as though ever since I'd met her, or him, I'd totally lost sight of my professional self, of this world of psychiatry I'd chosen to enter. I'd been going through the motions, and since I'm pretty darn smart for a southern boy, I had managed to get away with it. But there *you* were, or seemed to be, in the dark corner of an obscure Indian restaurant, as big as life and bringing all that life back to me in its full force and seriousness as well.

"I really admire you, Wayne, and for the first time I wondered what you, what any psychiatrist, would think of what I was doing, of what I had done, of how I had manipulated Darrell—for I saw suddenly that was the word for all my support. The thought pulled me out of myself, out of that phantasmic world, into the drab world of reality. But once you see the light, it's hard to go back—and maybe I really wanted out anyhow.

"As I say, I didn't want to know whether it was really you, and for the moment I put you out of my mind and settled down to enjoy the evening with Darlene. But the zest had gone out of things. I could feel that all the while she was chatting away, trying to amuse me. And I felt it even more that night in bed.

"Darlene came to me in one of the glamorous nightgowns I'd bought her, and I suddenly didn't see her anymore as the woman I loved and doted on but as a patient. A patient, for God's sake! Well, the thought just squashed all libidinal desire, as we say in the trade. Darlene was as sweet as cream, tried to reassure me as women do, saying it happens to everyone, that I must have had too much wine with dinner. And I bought it for the moment and tried to lose myself in her as I had for a month of nights. But no amount of kissing that skin as smooth as satin could keep me from thinking, She's a patient! She's a patient! In this trade, I know that's about as forbidden as it is to mess around in bed with a black woman where I come from. But then, I suppose," he added, "it's not worse than being a fairy.

"That night I realized I'd been living a dream, Wayne! A *dream!* From then on I couldn't get it up at all, but was afraid to tell Darlene why, and she began to think she wasn't enough of a woman for me. I recognized I'd been playing God in the worst way, but now I'd woken up to see I'd been playing a cruel joke on her! All the pain, all the hope, all her dreams. How was I going to deal with it? With her?

"I really tried hard to regain the feeling of professionalism I'd had those many months before when I'd first met Darrell. I told her we had to terminate our love affair, that it was no good, that it was wrong for both of us. Darlene went all to pieces when she heard me put it that way. The word "terminate" sounded all too ominous, as perhaps I'd meant it to. She moaned and cried and wouldn't get out of bed for days at a time. The tranquilizers and antidepressants I got her only dulled the pain a bit, but not the idea that terminating the relationship was a death of some kind, invalidating all that I had made of her."

"That means she hadn't made anything of herself?" I interjected mildly.

"I suppose I hadn't given her time to," Larry said, surprised. "We had our own world for that month and for a while that was enough. But now that I was trying to end it, the idea that she wasn't enough of a woman for me played through her mind again and again, obsessing her totally."

I was able to guess the rest of the story, Darlene's suicide attempt and Larry's ultimate rescue. There was more to come. But when I thought about it then, in the hours after Larry had initially recounted his story, I was struck again and again by the number of interlocking dreams and fantasies which had gone into the creation of this almost mythical mating. All psychiatrists worth their salt would acknowledge the fact that we have myriad fantasies about our patients. All of us have thought about them sexually at one time or another. It's hard to be as intimate emotionally with patients as psychiatrists have to be without desiring to share other intimacies with them as well. Only most of us don't act on our desires. We don't translate our fleeting fantasies into realities. We are trained to recognize them for what they are, so that we can set them aside. It's what you don't acknowledge in yourself, like Larry's desire for power, for sexual possession, that can screw up your life—to say nothing of the lives of other people and, if you are a psychiatrist, of the vulnerable men and women who depend on you to be clear-sighted on their behalf.

Clearly Larry had flouted all the treatment principles psychiatrists hold to be self-evident. It wasn't simply that he had lusted after a patient. It was the particular patient whom he had lusted after that made it such a problem. And the fact that he had kept it all to himself, consulting no one about that sex-change operation. Change is one thing, metamorphosis another, especially when you're going to catch the butterfly in your own net and pin it down forever. The bastard, I thought. How could he abuse her like that? And suddenly I was heaping judgment upon judgment on Larry, in a silent, furious indictment of his crimes against a person who had put her total trust, her very fragile life, into his hands for molding and safekeeping, only to find herself tossed aside in the end with nothing to hold on to. I only caught myself when I began cursing him aloud. Talk about judgmental therapists. I took the cake, I mused. Judgmentalism had no place here and would not solve Larry's and Darlene's problems, any more than it ever solves anyone's problems. That's the chief thing wrong with it, really: being judgmental makes you feel you're effective, when you really haven't tried to think a problem through at all.

I began to try to piece together just what Darrell/Darlene had meant to Larry. The ambiguous amalgam she had represented was the absolutely perfect fit for all the crazy holes in Larry's psyche, the final common pathway for the stuff of his dreams. She had the tall, thin body he had always craved and the warm black skin of the woman who had raised him when his mother was too busy playing tennis at the country club or serving tea at a charity bazaar. And she was forbidden, too, fulfilling his mother's expectation that he would always do the wrong thing. More than that, she was his own creation, the Galatea he had chiseled out of ebony skin and bone—an opportunity unheard of, undreamed of, or rather, appropriate only to dreams, to create a mate tailored solely for himself. And she had literally given him the opportunity to make a woman of her. She would forever adore him for that, forever be his slave.

He had freed the butterfly, rescued the woman tragically locked within the confines of a man's body. And he need not ever fear her, as he did the flirtatious girls who fluttered out of his reach at the glittering balls he had gone to as a young man. Darlene would always be there for him, always ready, always servile, always embodying the visions and virtues his mother had failed to live up to. Implicit in this last statement was evidence of the enormous increment of rage Larry had always carried within him toward his unavailable mother. What better way to avenge himself on her than to replace her with a black mammy, but one as lovely and lissome as any Georgia belle?

Finally, the fact that Darlene had once been a man clearly made her all the more exciting for Larry sexually, with its imprint of the forbidden and the ambiguous. In engineering his lover's castration, he had triumphed in fantasy over his father as well as his mother. In filling Darlene's virginal vagina with his penis, he brought to her, to them, what his parents had never brought to him. He became the perfect merger of man and woman. What more could anyone possibly dream of in a love than what Darrell/Darlene had to offer him?

But some dreams wake us from our sleep in terror. And Darlene's bleeding wrists proved to be the nightmare vision that was necessary to rouse Larry from his torpor. "I'm sorry" was all he could muster to say to her later when she awoke from her sleep after her attempt at suicide. He had no explanation to offer then, either to her or to himself. And when he told me that he and Darlene were still living together, I could see that he was more or less throwing himself on my mercy, hoping perhaps that I would rescue him as he had "rescued" Darlene. Or was it Darrell he had truly rescued, only to throw Darlene to the wolves?

I didn't know whether I wanted to go on with this supervision or not. Still, I did keep Larry's next appointment. When he came in, he told me how Darlene had spent most of the week lying in bed, her face turned to the wall, not speaking to him and eating the most minimal amount of food. "And I sit there beside her, hoping she'll lash out at me, vilify, anything . . ."

"Why do you think you do that?" I asked.

"Oh, I don't know," he said, a bit shamefaced. "My guilty conscience, I suppose."

"Hoping she'll exonerate you?" I couldn't help asking dryly, but Larry was too sunk in self-abasement to notice.

Then he said he had told Darlene that he had consulted me, and that roused her. The upshot was that she had asked him to arrange a psychiatric consultation for her with me.

"Why?" I asked, startled.

"I don't really understand, but she seems to think some impartial observer might help her, and since you already know about the case it's easier than if she had to go over all this shit with someone else."

While I had my reservations about how much I could really help Darlene, I agreed to see her because her notion about the usefulness of an impartial observer seemed a good one, a healthy perception. One that rather surprised me. But then Larry had really told me very little about the real Darlene.

I have to admit that I was curious to see her. Who was this person Larry had created? A figment of his fantasies or a woman with a life of her own?

She turned out to be all that Larry had said, beautiful and poised. But she was more. She was a gentle woman, thoughtful and reserved, not the distraught creature I had anticipated from Larry's description. Darlene was the person she wanted to be, as I realized when I met her. Larry clearly was not. I saw her only twice and a few minutes before the end of our second session, we had reached a stopping point. Gathering up her bag, Darlene said, "You've been most helpful, Wayne, and I've come to a decision. I'm leaving New York."

"Where will you go?" I asked.

"Larry's given me some money, and I'm going to find myself a nice middle-sized city to live in and then go back and finish school. And after that, I'm thinking of becoming a social worker. I feel I might have a real talent for understanding the suffering of other people, having been through enough myself."

Darlene shook hands with me gravely and left. I never heard from her again. But judging by her persistence in going after what she felt she needed in order to live a full life, I would expect that she has survived, and survived well. As little as it was evident in Larry's report of her, she struck me as a person with the strength to overcome adversity.

Larry was another story. In later sessions, he filled me in on the details of his past. He had left his therapist, he said, because he felt that he could not talk to her about what he had been planning with Darrell. When he told me her name, however, I was surprised. I knew her to be an intelligent, compassionate woman.

After we worked for some weeks on Larry's feelings about the devastation he felt he had inflicted on Darlene and on himself, he asked me to take him on as a regular patient. I said no. In spite of his lively intelligence, I sensed in him a trouble I wasn't sure I wanted to deal with, all the implications perhaps of that overbearing southern colonel struggling for control. And for all his eagerness, Larry still had some crucial reservations about me. I finally told him I felt he needed a fresh face and that the renegotiation of our relationship would not be in his best interests. A rather formal termination, but there was something about Larry, some triviality behind his courtliness, that brought out this stance in me.

I wondered for a long time whether I really believed what I

had said to Larry. Did I really think it was not possible to switch over from the more remote supervisory to the closer therapeutic role? I was uncertain about the answer. And then I thought of Darlene. Larry's manipulation of her was more than I could stomach. I could not help being judgmental where Larry was concerned. I had thought I liked him when the supervision began. Now I was not so sure. You do not have to like every aspect of a patient, but therapy is hard going if you are constantly struggling to suppress your reservations about some character flaw.

I saw to it that Larry got another therapist. From then on, whenever we ran into each other at a psychiatric meeting, we would shake hands and politely ask how the other was doing. Only I think that neither one of us really wanted to know. We both wanted to be free of each other.

Then I heard that Larry had come out of the closet during his therapy. He became very successful as a psychiatrist to gays, until he contracted AIDS. He died a couple of years ago, and when I heard the news I felt a pang of responsibility. Maybe I should have become his therapist. Maybe things would have worked out in a different way and he would still be alive. But then I caught myself. Wasn't that the very dream Larry had, of having a god's power to change the lives of others? Perhaps it was a fantasy I was subject to as well.

Larry had lived out what most of us have only flirted with for moments at a time. It was not white bread he wanted to live on but wedding cake. With that realization, I knew I had been right in not taking him on as a patient. And I believe now that something in that possibility frightened me. Could I have feared that I, too, might have succumbed to the temptation to be Pygmalion?

CHAPTER 2

*The Dream
of
Revenge*

What happens when a therapist treats a famous person—
a star? Does the therapist behave differently? And what if the
therapist herself is the child of a star? An unusual situation, I
admit, but one that, as in the case of Alicia, illustrates a central problem in therapy—the problem I call the dream of revenge.

This young therapist had called me out of the blue one day.
She told me a bit about herself. After taking her doctorate in
psychology at one of our leading schools and spending half a
dozen years working for various mental health agencies, she
had decided to branch out on her own and set up a private
practice. She worked mostly with young people who were
having trouble establishing just who they were and what they
wanted to do with their lives. But Alicia also had an occasional
older patient. "And now I've got this old woman I just can't
crack," she told me. "I know your book on the psychotherapy
of the elderly and it made me think you might be just the
person to help me."

The book was one I had written in 1984 to counteract the
prevailing wisdom that said the prescription pad is the only
sure way to deal with emotionally unstable old people. Therapy is a waste, so the party line ran, since the old are essentially incurable, too many neurons having dropped off into the

nitrogen pool for any real mental change to be possible. Or there was not time enough to treat the old before they die. And so on and so on. From my observation of therapists, however, I had become convinced that their reluctance to treat the elderly was not all that rational. Rather, it grew out of unresolved feelings about a parent or even a former therapist.

Alicia's eagerness and interest in the subject made me think it could be rewarding to work with her. So we made an appointment to have her come to my office to discuss the idea of my supervising her. When she arrived, she turned out to be as attractive as she sounded. Tall, with a swinging, confident stride, a mass of dark flyaway hair, and curiously light eyes, she looked no more than thirty, although with her experience I knew she had to be some years older. But I was caught by more than the good looks. In her walk and the set of her eyes, there was something familiar, haunting, as if I had known her before. But where? Not in any ordinary context, that was certain.

Alicia sat right down and plunged into the case of her patient Myra, who was seventy years old. "There's something unsettling about her—was from the very beginning," she said. "A strange mixture of hesitancy and condescension that's off-putting, though I'm not sure why. It's as if she is some grande dame to whom I owe obeisance. But she's just a gimpy old lady dressed in dark Yves Saint Laurent suits, that military tunic look everyone was wearing in the late sixties and seventies.

"The first time I met her, I was struck by her voice," Alicia continued. "It's jarring, high-pitched and squeaky, completely unexpected in a woman with the sort of ramrod carriage she manages in spite of her arthritis. She simply announced that she was depressed and then stopped there, as if I was supposed to fill in the gaps from my imagination or to know exactly what it was that was bothering her. There's something extraordinarily irritating about that manner of hers—though, to give the devil her due, words are certainly not her primary means of communication. Nor ever were."

Alicia said that as if I must automatically know what Myra's primary means of communication was. She did not, however, elaborate, but went right ahead presenting the case. "It was like pulling teeth to find out that Myra was suffering from the usual signs of a major depression—the early morning waking, the appetite and weight loss, the whole thing. She seemed to equate each and every admission with some sign of weakness, some fatal flaw in the picture she wanted to project to me. It was as if her entire universe rested on the fulcrum of the image she was giving me of herself. You can't imagine how hard it was to take!"

I wondered about Alicia as I listened. Myra's narcissism was rubbing her as raw as if the old woman were her mother.

"And in the weeks I've been seeing her, she's not responded to therapy at all! No matter what we've said in a session, or what she's agreed to do, she just leaves my office and goes back home and moons and waits for her daughter to call. She's just stagnating!"

I agreed to supervise Alicia's handling of the case and we scheduled another appointment. There are a number of ways to handle a supervision. You can be formal and ask the supervisee to bring in process notes of sessions with patients, made either during or after a session, and then discuss a technical problem such as how to deal with certain kinds of patients, or such issues as insufficiently worked-out sexist feelings that get in the way of treatment. Or you can be informal and have the supervisee leave pen and notebook at home and speak about a patient off the cuff. I prefer the latter method, as it lets the patient be filtered through the supervisee's own unconscious. If you're lucky, you get the essence of both patient and therapist.

During her next appointment, Alicia quickly bogged down in this approach. She would start out, her voice strong, to describe a session, but then she would hesitate, her voice dropping to a whisper, and begin to hop from one detail to another. Finally, she would be all scrambled up, coherence long lost. In desperation, she would turn to her notes, but even

SHRINK DREAMS

they were of little use. "It's all a blank," she finally said during another appointment, after she had simply been listing a series of Myra's actions without a hint of what they meant to the old woman or how she herself felt about them. "I don't understand it. I've never had this kind of trouble with a patient—to say nothing of a supervision. It grosses me out, as one of my yuppie patients might say!" and she laughed nervously.

"Do you think it's something particular about Myra?" I asked." Or about presenting her to me?"

"It can't have anything to do with you, Wayne," she said emphatically. "No, it's got to be something about *her*. Only I have no idea what."

Alicia's initial description of Myra had struck me as bland and empty. The woman was depressed and obviously needed to be roused into some constructive activity. But what was so unusual about that? If it weren't for the obvious block Alicia was reporting in treating her, I would have wondered why she had chosen to discuss Myra's case at all. I had discovered that Alicia was well grounded in both psychodynamic theory and the problems of the aged. So I had to conclude that her difficulties with Myra arose from unresolved countertransference issues in her own life, issues to which I as yet had no clue. I told myself I would just have to be patient and wait for the source of trouble to reveal itself. "Murder will out" is a first principle of therapy.

"I'm sure the problem is that Myra makes me feel I'm a rotten therapist," Alicia said another day. "And she's not even that depressed anymore."

"Oh?" I said.

"She's not really showing the vegetative signs she had to start with."

In Myra's case, the physiological symptoms that accompanied her depression were loss of appetite and weight, waking up in the early morning and being unable to go back to sleep, difficulty in concentration, and loss of libidinal interest. I knew that it was probably the antidepressant medication Myra was taking that had diminished those symptoms, without in any way diminishing the old woman's lifelong problems, which were proving so difficult for Alicia to deal with in therapy.

"Ever since her husband died," Alicia continued, "Myra just lets herself blob out in those designer suits of hers. It's as if she's given up on life. I like older people," she said, almost defensively, "but I guess I find that attitude hard to take."

"Yes," I said, "she does seem to have a sort of malaise that blots out her perception of any sunlight entering her life."

Alicia went on to tell me about Myra's relationship with her husband, whom she had married in her early thirties. Stephen was an orthopedic surgeon who had done a lot of work with famous athletes. "Myra told me they weren't all that close early in their marriage. It was as if they were orbiting in separate galaxies, as she says."

"And she had children?" I prompted.

"Only one, a daughter, when she was nearly forty." And now Alicia straightened, her voice hardening. "It's obvious Myra didn't have much use for being a mother or a homemaker. A whole slew of servants managed everything for her, including her baby girl. So Stella, that's her daughter's name, didn't see her much."

This clearly bothered Alicia, but before I had a chance to say anything she went on to tell me that when the daughter was seven and the couple had been married a dozen years, they started to spend more time together. "And as they got more dependent on each other, they left their Stella even more in the cold."

I still wanted to pick up on the daughter, but again Alicia turned back to the couple. "Frankly, though they were clearly mutually dependent, I think Myra needed Stephen more than he needed her. He buoyed her up, gave her an audience she could always count on." I noticed that Alicia said this as if it was the last thing she could ever be counted on for.

Then she told me that Myra had begun to suffer from arthritis in her early sixties. The disease affected her feet most of all and slowly but surely eroded her mobility and her capacity to enjoy traveling with her husband. It also affected her overall mood, plummeting her into the first of a series of depressive episodes during which she could not eat or sleep. Ultimately she had sought help from physicians or psychiatrists, who prescribed medication in the time-honored way. It was no surprise to me to hear that while the variety of antidepressant drugs prescribed for her over the years had helped ease her psychic suffering, they had not enabled her to pick up the pieces of what appeared to have been an active life. In desperation, Myra had turned to more dynamically oriented therapists. But at this point, her depression was crucially exacerbated when her husband died suddenly from a heart attack.

"She slipped into a really horrendous black mood," Alicia said. "Wouldn't eat, wasn't hungry, couldn't sleep, her thoughts skittering around like water in a hot frying pan. Her doctor gave her that big new antidepressant which was being written up everywhere. And it did help her regain her appetite and sleep straight through the night. But she still saw little real purpose in her life. And that's when I came into the picture," Alicia said. "When her daughter's doctor suggested that she see me."

The daughter again, so casually mentioned. Although she was evidently so little a part of the mother's life, it had been through her that Myra had gone to Alicia. At last Alicia had paused, giving me a chance to ask about Stella's relationship with Myra.

"That's the big mystery," Alicia said, wryly. "I can tell she's not enamored of her mother. From what Myra says, Stella is really grudging about visiting her. As if coming to see her is a dose of medicine she's forced to take. Just like when I was a child and I'd screw myself up inside and swallow down as fast as possible the awful-tasting castor oil my nanny used to give me."

Alicia's association to her own childhood didn't escape me, but I only asked why she thought Stella had been so negative about her mother.

"Oh," said Alicia, throwing up her hands with a charming smile, as if it didn't really matter. "I haven't made any headway there at all."

"Have you thought about contacting Stella herself, getting her to help Myra and even solve the mystery?"

"I don't really think I should," Alicia said, her usually mobile expression set hard. "Don't you think," she went on, throwing the problem back at me, her low voice raised to a pitch of falseness, "that Myra would see it as intruding on the confidentiality of our relationship?"

"Well," I said mildly, pondering her transparent lack of sincerity, "you'd only do it, of course, if Myra was willing." Certainly Alicia knew as well as I did that bringing in one or more family members has long been used as an adjunctive technique in the treatment of the elderly.

After Alicia left that day and over the next week, I struggled to make some sense of the muddled picture she had given me of the relationship between Myra and her daughter. Just who is this woman Myra, I wondered? She sounded like a burned-out narcissist, I thought, Probably her own mother wasn't attuned to her as a child, didn't mirror her moods appropriately, so that she could never find herself reflected in her mother and feel herself really confirmed and cared for. Say a child brings its mother a bunch of dandelions one day, and the mother frowns and turns away and snaps, "Oh, those are just weeds! Throw them away!" And say the child's offerings are responded to thus again and again. Such a child is likely to grow up with a drastically curtailed sense of self, one so focused on oneself as to leave little room for others' needs. Could this be Myra's problem? Had only her gifts been seen and not herself? And what *was* her gift? What had been the essence of her life? Of this important factor, I realized Alicia had still conveyed no idea.

There were all too many other unanswered questions to which Alicia had not provided answers. Why did Myra marry so late? Why did she wait so long to have children? Why only one? But wasn't Myra herself an only child? Yes, I was certain

Alicia had said she was. So Myra had probably actively visited upon her daughter what she had passively experienced with her own mother. She had gained belated mastery by bringing misery to another. Identification with the aggressor is what we call it in the trade. The golden rule of child rearing as practiced by a narcissist's mother: Do Unto Others What Others Have Done Unto You—no matter how bad. And double the dose if you can.

And so on to more questions. What did Myra do for those thirty-four years before she married Stephen? Why hadn't Alicia told me about them? In reporting on her treatment of Myra, she had just been giving me the mechanics of who said this and that, the phenomenon of the sessions rather than their emotional meat and potatoes. And her circumlocutions didn't amount to a damn thing! But why hadn't I asked her for more? Either I was succumbing to her obvious admiration for me, or my blind spots must have been in tune with hers.

That latter possibility led me to realize that Alicia had to be struggling with some deep-seated countertransference feeling, some poignant pain she had suffered at the hands of an older woman, maybe her mother. My mother had some narcissistic features of her own, although she was certainly not anything like the pure culture of it I imagined Myra's mother to have been. But what, then, about *Alicia's* mother? That might not be a bad question to ask. The more I thought about it, the more I saw I would have to ambush Alicia in some way out of her circumlocutions. And jog *myself* out of accepting them.

When Alicia came in the next week, I gave her a few moments before I pounced. Maybe during the week a miracle had occurred, and she would be capable of presenting her case in another way. "I had something of a revelation about Myra this week," she announced. "I think she equates getting better with giving me something, and she'll be damned if she'll do that no matter how much she hurts herself by holding back."

That opening sentence would have made me feel better

about Alicia's understanding of Myra, had it not been for the tone of her voice. It dripped venom, revealing her inability to use whatever insight she might have gained.

"Myra told me that the manager of the local senior citizens center had invited her to put on a dance performance," Alicia went on, "and she refused him point-blank. She could do it with both hands tied behind her back!"

"What do you mean?" I asked, hastily putting out of my mind the ludicrous picture of the tiny, well-coiffed woman Alicia had described in such a situation.

"Didn't I ever tell you?" she said in a resigned sort of way. "Myra was a prima ballerina in her youth."

Only then did I attach a last name to the first name I had heard so many times. Myra Allison. One of the spangled names of the international world of ballet. "So that's why she married so late," I murmured, although I had never actually wondered about it to Alicia.

"Of course!" she snapped back, once again losing her composure. "You couldn't expect her to give up all that adulation from her audiences several nights a week just to marry some man who'd swell her belly with a brood of brats and break the magic link with the bravos and the flowers! You couldn't expect her to do that, could you?"

I stared at the attractive woman in the chair opposite me. How could she have left this enormous piece of the puzzle out of our sessions for so long? Myra was no simple homebound hausfrau suffering from bereavement or the empty-nest syndrome. She had once been a peerless star outshining all competition, until her age and arthritis brought her down. And now she could no longer command the adulation of audiences, but had to watch other stars receiving it. How could Alicia have simply left all that out of her story? There had to be a damned good reason.

"I'm really surprised to hear all this, Alicia," I said. "Why didn't you mention it to me before?"

"It didn't occur to me that it mattered all that much," she said with a smile, trying to sustain her air of insouciance.

"Maybe it wouldn't matter in general that she was one of the greatest ballerinas of all time, but *here* I think it does. It's central to her story."

Alicia just looked at me, the smile quite gone.

"Why are you so angry at her?" I asked.

"I'm not angry at her. I'm angry at you."

"At me?"

"Yes, you," she said, her tone icy. Then she stared at me haughtily. "I never thought you'd be a star-fucker, Wayne. It's unbecoming."

My own anger surged. The presumption of this woman jumping on me like that! But before I totally lost my temper, my professional self wondered whether I might not really be into star-fucking. At the same moment, it allowed the thought to surface that Alicia was not indicting me. It was someone else. Someone from her own past. Some ghost that had not been exorcised was rattling its bones resentfully.

I took a deep breath and let my anger subside. Then I said quietly, not knowing what might come next, "Alicia, I think you're trying to shoot someone down, but it's not me."

Her eyes blazed and I braced myself for an outburst. But her gaze dropped and she began to cry.

"You're right," she murmured. Then her control gave way and the tears came. She couldn't speak for a moment. "I'll be all right in a minute," she said finally, trying to smile. "Just let me be until I get it together again."

"No problem," I replied. "Take all the time you need."

When Alicia finally managed to compose herself and began to speak, she was a different person. Her husky voice had lost its old hesitation and become authoritative. Even the contours of her face altered, and then I recognized in them what had first haunted me about her looks.

"Practically every man I've ever known, from my father on down, has always been more interested in my mother than in me," she said. "You know who I mean, don't you, Wayne? Valerie Young, the late, great movie queen." Again scorn was seeping into her voice.

I nodded. I didn't want to interrupt her.

"My father was her first husband, one of those Beverly Hills doctors to the stars. That's how they met. She had a sore throat, or a case of hot pants is my guess, he being famous for his bedside, if not bed, manners. He made a house call and never left.

"The studio gave the marriage its blessing. Mother was something of a hell-raiser and the bigwigs down at the lot thought my father would be a stabilizing influence. What did they know? At the time she was as magical off-screen as on— and she had no trouble *de*stabilizing him.

"Then a couple of her pictures bombed and the publicity people thought it would be a good idea for Vivacious Val— that's what my father called her after they split—to have a little baby to rev up audience interest. 'Isn't she darling?' Mother cooed over me when she cuddled me in front of the TV cameras. But when the reporters and photographers left, she handed me back to my nanny. Valerie Young wasn't much into mothering."

"When she split up with Daddy, I didn't get to see her much. He got custody of me, long before it became fashionable for fathers to do that. I'd see my mother with one or another of her husbands in Europe occasionally or on some ski slope, but most of the time she didn't want to be reminded of, even own up to, my existence. And the only way I could think of getting even with her was by never watching one of her films. How's that for identification with the aggressor?"

I just nodded, feeling it was wise to let her get out the painful feelings she had bottled up for so long.

"I don't think I cried much when she went away and left me with my father. It was hard to tell the difference. I know I sound bitter, and I guess I am. I thought I was over most of it. I've spent the better part of my life in one sort of treatment or another. But some things hurt forever."

She stopped and I let the silence grow until she was ready to fill it.

"From the outside looking in, it must seem wonderful to

have a movie star for a mother. On the inside though, it's not so hot. Even if articles about your mother in the tabloids can shoot up your rating with some people, it's the pits for your self-esteem or for getting real friends or decent men. As is the fact that she doesn't ever really want to see you while she's alive, to say nothing of having her go and *kill* herself."

Alicia's reference to her mother's suicide evoked for me the stark images, the wreckage of the car, the burned mountainside I had seen on TV at the time. Even more, the eerie parallel between Valerie Young driving her Ferrari off a cliff and the famous death scene in one of her movies crowded out thoughts of Alicia for a moment. What a fan I had been of her mother's films. I was certain I had seen all of them at least once and some of them probably half a dozen times. Maybe, I pulled myself up short, there was something to that starfucking accusation of Alicia's.

But Alicia had pulled herself together and was going on. "I've never been able to reconcile the reality of Valerie Young with the mothers other girls had. She was hardly what the textbooks describe as the average expectable mother. And, of course, neither was Myra. When she was referred to me, I didn't know who she was at first. And she didn't mention it. Then one day she started talking about her dancing and suddenly sitting right where she was I saw my own mother batting those famous pale eyes of hers, and I wanted to slam out of there and leave both of them. But then I thought it might be good for me to try to treat Myra. Maybe it would help me come to terms with all the garbage from the past. Only it didn't work out that way. My empathy went out to her daughter, not to Myra.

"God, I hate that bitch!" Alicia said, banging her clenched fists on the arms of the chair. "All she ever cared about was her goddamn career, her fucking dancing. She never gave a bloody damn about her child. Admirers all over the world tossed bouquets over the footlights to her, but did she ever toss one lousy kiss to her baby girl? Did she rock her and hug her? Sit up with her at night when she was sick? Help her grow up? Well, I'll be damned if I'm going to toss her anything in treatment! She can rot in hell before I'll help her get well. I'd like to see her die of her depression the way Vivacious Val did! Only this time it'll be under my control, not hers! That's better than nothing!"

As I listened to Alicia, watched her distorted face, I wondered whether we could salvage any of her treatment. The outlook was chancy. Alicia posed a special case for a supervising therapist. I could not tell her to go back to her analyst or therapist and try to deal with the issues she had raised, as she was not then in treatment and hadn't been for some years. I would certainly recommend that she start seeing someone right away, but would that help soon enough to rescue the treatment with Myra, assuming it could even *be* rescued?

I decided that it might help Alicia if I jumped out of my role as a supervisor into that of a therapist for a moment, and made a few interpretations of my own. "Anyone who tells you revenge isn't sweet," I began, "is full of crap. And I believe you deserve all the revenge you can get. But you're much too smart to allow these feelings to take over your life, to destroy your effectiveness with a patient. Maybe being a lousy mother-therapist to Myra is a way of holding on to your own lousy mother, a derivative of the something-is-better-than-nothing school. Only if you do that, Alicia, you never let yourself grow up. You have to let go sometime.

"One last thing. No matter what you consciously thought, you must have known that you and I would eventually get to this point. And you must have wanted that or you would never have called me in to supervise your treatment of Myra. If you really hated her and wanted nothing but revenge, you would have quietly let her die off through the ineffectiveness of the treatment, and no one would have been the wiser. Only some part of you must have wanted something more, some sort of resolution of the past."

I looked her straight in the eyes. "Pay attention to that part,

Alicia, and give yourself a break! Doing your best with Myra's treatment now is the single most important thing you can do for your own life."

I could see that Alicia *was* hearing me. She was clearly trying hard not to cry.

"There's just one more thing I want you to do," I added. "Go out and rent two or three of your mother's movies and watch them tonight. Especially *Deirdre*, where she drives the car off the cliff. It's time to stop denying that she existed as a star. And if you can accept that, you might be able to accept Myra, too."

Our time was up and as Alicia rose from the chair, I told her I would contact her later that day with the name of a therapist she might see. Later, unable to reach her directly, I left the therapist's name and telephone number on her answering machine.

When Alicia returned the following week, she announced that she was going back into treatment with the person I had recommended. "It's been a tough few days," she said, "but I think I've learned a lot."

I guessed she had been through five different kinds of hell the past week, but she seemed calmer and more at ease with herself.

"I want to thank you for what you said to me last week. Especially the part about hanging on to my own lousy mother by being a lousy mother-therapist to Myra. You were right. And the part about watching Mother's films. It was uncanny. I didn't know whether to scream or cry when I watched *Deirdre*. I must have looked at it five or six times. The first couple of times I covered my eyes when she drives the car over the cliff. It was too close for comfort. Then gradually I could let myself look at it. The biggest surprise for me was recognizing just how great she was in the film and in the others I watched. She could express so many nuances of feeling, feelings I never dreamed she had in her. Why couldn't she have brought them out with me?"

"It's good you were able to feel that, Alicia," I said. "And how did it go with Myra this week?"

"Not terrifically. When I'm with her, I keep drifting back and forth between the present and the past. Half the time I see my mother's face staring back at me, with all that makeup on. Do you know I never saw her without it? And I still want to kill her. I'm not sure I can get past that."

"Give it a little time."

"I'll try."

And try she and Myra did, over many months. It was not a treatment that went easily. But it did progress. And with each forward step Myra made, Alicia seemed softer and less angry.

About a year or so later, Myra finally did accept an invitation to stage a dance program at the senior citizens center. She worked on it for weeks, tirelessly coaching the men and women who were limber enough to perform. A week before the gala evening, she invited both Alicia and her daughter, Stella, to attend. Alicia came in the day after the performance and told me about it.

"I wish you could have been there, Wayne!" she said, her eyes shining as they never had in all the time I had been supervising her. "The performance was a triumph and it was all Myra's doing. She got all those old men and women to waltz and twirl and bow, even with one quite presentable *grand jeté*. And all so graceful and gallant you forgot how decrepit some of them are. It was positively inspiring.

"And at the end, when the dancers had taken their final bows, the audience kept on clapping and shouting for Myra until finally she came out and ever so slowly and painfully mounted the steps to the stage. There the manager of the center presented her with a bouquet of yellow roses. After dropping him a royal curtsy, and hugging and kissing him on both cheeks, she looked out over the audience to the two seats in the middle of the front row where Stella and I were sitting. Plucking two roses from her bouquet, she whispered a few words to the manager. And Wayne, I wish you could have seen the tender look on her face as she watched him walk down the steps and over to us and then, with a little bow, present each of us with one of those roses.

CHAPTER 3

The Dream of Being White

T he question of what happens when a therapist treats a patient whose cultural or ethnic background is very different from his or her own is one of those submerged issues that is rarely confronted. Few therapists readily admit that racial stereotypes and fantasies play a part in interracial therapy, but they most certainly do. Black-white therapy can be particularly problematic, since racism is a pervasive force in our society and we all have fixed ideas of what it means to be black or white. When therapist and patient are of different races, these issues have to be addressed. If a therapist tries to be "color-blind," the therapy suffers.

Joyce was a black therapist who insisted on this particular fiction about her feelings toward a white patient. It masked a powerful countertransference dream—the dream of being white. Yet Joyce, a proud, accomplished, and independent black woman, was the last person who would have suspected herself of harboring this dream. And her lack of insight made her patient a pawn of the dream.

Joyce first contacted me because she heard me speak on interracial therapy. My lecture brought to mind an impasse she had reached in treating a young woman, she told me on the telephone. Although she doubted that race had anything to do with it, she was nevertheless asking for my supervision.

After this rather odd statement, she dropped the subject of race altogether, telling me neither her own race nor that of her patient.

I was not surprised, however, when Joyce turned out to be black. Her velvet contralto voice and melodious intonation had given me a hint that she might be. Ever since I was a small child, I have been fascinated with voices. I remember listening to my mother and trying to figure out what her various intonations implied. Was she angry or sad? Had I done the right thing or upset her? A voice, I learned early, could provide valuable clues to what a person was about. When I set up an appointment with Joyce, I wondered if her personality would match the pleasant promise of her voice. It did.

Joyce, I quickly discovered, was one of those people whose warmth instantly puts others at ease. After only a few moments of chatter about the weather and the difficulties of getting around in New York, I felt I had known her a long time. Moreover, she seemed to have the ability to listen and empathize that is so important in a therapist.

She was attractive to look at, too, tall and slender, with beautiful skin and high cheekbones. Her thick hair was cropped close to her head, emphasizing the oval shape of her face. But it was her obvious flair for fashion that was most notable. Joyce wore a two-piece tweed ensemble of orange and brown, the top of which was a poncholike affair, secured with a belt. It had soft gold fringes that matched her gold hoop earrings and the muted gold specks in her brown shoes. When she saw me looking at her outfit, Joyce commented that she had designed it herself. "I used to have my own boutique," she said, "with all my own creations."

The boutique, Foxes at Work, had been located in a middle-class black neighborhood in Queens where Joyce lived. "The idea," she told me, "was to have unique clothing that would go straight from the office to dinner or some other social event. Like these duds, for example. I'm going to a cocktail sip as soon as I leave here."

For all of Joyce's originality, Foxes at Work had closed

some time ago. The rent got too high, the debt too large, and truth to tell, Joyce told me, she was ready for another career, or more accurately to go back to her first career, psychology. She enrolled in an excellent training program to get additional certification, and for two years had been working at a private psychotherapy center on the West Side. She also saw several private patients, and was interested in having more. "I want my own practice," she commented. "I'm an entrepreneurial type, and I like being on my own. I guess I'm just used to taking care of myself."

Joyce summarized her background succinctly. She came from a working-class family, she said. Her father, a sanitation worker, left her mother when Joyce was quite small and her mother worked as a housekeeper in "other folk's houses." I noticed that Joyce was careful not to note the color of the people who owned the other houses or to express any resentment at her mother's circumstances.

Joyce did well in school, and in spite of her mother's small income, she went on to college and graduate school. She financed her education by waiting on tables and selling cosmetics door to door. Joyce described her relationship with her mother as "distant." She never seemed to be able to listen to what Joyce was telling her. But in spite of the coolness between them, she had been greatly upset when her mother died a few years previously.

What she and her mother had in common, Joyce said, was that they were both independent women. Joyce was proud of her capacity to manage on her own. I could see she didn't like asking for help, but now she was "stumped" by a difficult problem with a patient. Since she first came to see Joyce, this young woman, who had had trouble breaking away from her family, had fallen in love with a man but was frightened of losing her virginity. Joyce didn't seem to be able to help her resolve this conflict.

The patient, Cindy Morrison, came from an upper-middle-class white family in a prosperous New Jersey suburb. Her father was an attorney, her mother a full-time homemaker.

Joyce described the Morrisons as a "Dick and Jane" family, with a white house, a wide green lawn, a weekly gardener, a daily cleaning lady, a sauna, and two Mercedes, among other "toys." One of the toys was Cindy, the youngest of two children and the only girl. She had recently graduated from a community college, but when Joyce first met her, Cindy looked more like a junior high school student. She was only five feet tall, small-boned, and she wore what Joyce called "little girl clothes," blouses with bows, straight skirts, and flat shoes.

And Cindy was just as cute as her clothes, Joyce said. She had a heart-shaped face, an upturned nose, and big blue eyes. She looked like a doll, and that was what her family wanted her to be. Since she was a tiny baby, they had called her "Dolly" or "the doll." Her father had desperately wanted a daughter, and when he got one, he made her his pet. Cindy had been pampered and indulged from day one. She got everything she wanted, even before she knew she wanted it.

Fortunately, Joyce said, Cindy had a sweet nature; otherwise, she could have been made into an "impossible brat." Her problem was literally that she was too good. All her life, she had done pretty much what her parents expected her to, and she let them make her decisions. Her brother, on the other hand, had been encouraged to be independent.

"So little Cindy went into treatment because she wanted to be more independent, too?" I asked.

"You got it," Joyce replied. "She told me she needed to 'separate' from her family."

A previous attempt to separate had failed. Rather than commute to college as her parents wanted, Cindy had insisted on attending the University of Delaware, where many of her friends went. At Delaware, Cindy had come out of her shell a bit. She joined a sorority, started to mix with different types of people, and became a fashion design major, even though her father pronounced the subject "silly." But despite her progress, Cindy was frightened to be away from home. Her heart was in her mouth all the time, she said. And although she yearned for sexual experience, she was too timid to have any.

Like many people who are overly dependent on their parents, Cindy told her parents everything. She told them all about her roommate—when she slept in the dorm room with her boyfriend, when she became pregnant, and when she decided to have an abortion. At this juncture, Mr. Morrison insisted on pulling "the doll" out of the university and having her enroll at the community college nearby. Cindy felt more relief at being home than she dared admit, and in gratitude for feeling safe, she went along with her father's idea that she switch her major to secretarial studies.

With her two-year degree, Cindy had been working as a word processor in a nearby bank, where her family was well known. But six months ago, she had begun to resent the fact that her father had forced her to leave the university. She went to see Joyce with the notion of getting the emotional support she needed for a decision to return to Delaware for a four-year degree. Her parents opposed this idea, and deep down, Cindy feared they might be able to dissuade her. She had trouble, she said, standing up for her own decisions.

"She seems to have been able to make the decision to go into treatment all right," I remarked.

Joyce nodded. "She sure did, and it wasn't easy. Her father fought hard. But when he saw she had her heart set on it, he asked his internist to recommend a psychiatrist. He thought he was indulging her, of course. Anyway, the doctor came up with a noted name, but Cindy said no. She wanted to pick her own therapist."

Cindy found her in a fairly roundabout way, Joyce said. She had a friend at Delaware whose mother happened to have been Joyce's partner in the boutique. When Cindy told her friend she wanted to go into therapy, Joyce's name came up. Cindy came to interview Joyce, and after taking one look, said she wanted Joyce to treat her.

"Any idea why?"

My question was a pointed one. Whenever a person of one

race chooses a therapist of another, there's an unspoken reason as well as the given one. Usually, the silent reason has to do with a racial stereotype. A white man may want a black man to treat him, for example, because he's anxious to obtain a quality he associates with blacks, such as greater sexual potency, heightened aggressiveness, or increased self-reliance. A black man may seek out a white therapist because he thinks of whites as more powerful and therefore able to help him maneuver in a white-dominated world.

But for every stereotype the patient sees as positive, there's a negative buried somewhere, too. For example, the patient who hopes to become more aggressive with the help of a black therapist may also view blacks as potentially violent. So he might harbor a fear of the therapist. That's why, in interracial therapy, the therapist always has to be alert to what his background means to the patient. Positive stereotypes surface fairly easily because they flatter the therapist and reassure the patient. The negatives are more likely to remain buried and to cause problems.

Joyce was well aware of what I was getting at. She had made a point of asking Cindy why she selected her. Cindy said she admired the way black women could take care of themselves. That was something she longed to be able to do. She also shared Joyce's interest in fashion design, and she fantasized about having her own business some day. "I want to be just like you," she had said. So the therapeutic alliance was sealed.

Joyce knew what Cindy thought about her background—at least she knew the positives—but I wondered what she thought of Cindy and the Morrisons. Interracial therapy is very much a two-way street. The therapist has to realize that his or her notions of the patient may also be affected by racial beliefs. I suspected that Joyce might have strong emotions about rich white folks, particularly since her mother had been a servant in their houses. But when I suggested we discuss this, she insisted there was nothing to talk about. "I've come to terms with my feelings," she said. "I realize that there are bigots around, but I don't dwell on them. Basically, I try to see people as people."

"Sounds pretty noble, but I wonder how realistic it is," I commented.

Joyce was silent. I made a mental note that she seemed to be blocking what she might see in Cindy's whiteness. At some point, the issue would come up again. Perhaps we would be able to discuss it more frankly when she knew me better.

Meanwhile, we returned to what Joyce thought was important: the effect of Joyce's color on Cindy. Since Cindy idealized black women, a strong positive transference had been created, and Cindy had been able to go much further, much faster than even Joyce would have believed possible when treatment began six months ago.

Cindy had originally planned to reapply to Delaware, but after a number of sessions with Joyce, she realized that what she really wanted was to get a job in Manhattan. Going back to school would be a return to babyhood, she concluded. Through the woman who had referred her to Joyce, Cindy secured a job with a manufacturer of a "petite" clothing line. Her goal was to learn the fashion business. She was a receptionist and secretary, and unknown to her parents, she also did a little showroom modeling. Cindy was living alone in an apartment in Hoboken, just across the Hudson River from her job.

Given her previous history, Cindy's achievements were remarkable. They were so dramatic that I couldn't help wondering whether they stemmed from real change or from what we call a "transference cure." In a transference cure, the patient makes changes based on the strength of the relationship with the therapist rather than on his or her own growth. It's a matter of external versus internal, and a transference cure isn't likely to hold up over time, because the patient's internal conflicts remain unresolved. Eventually, they resurface.

Perhaps that would happen to Cindy, I thought. She was in a work situation that had to be anxiety-producing for her. The atmosphere in a clothing manufacturing firm can be chaotic and openly sexual. It bothered me that Cindy had found the job through the same woman who connected her to Joyce. And how had she found the apartment? Well, Joyce had simply mentioned that she knew many young people who liked living in Hoboken, and that rents were cheaper than in Manhattan. Then she and Cindy reviewed the various ways one found an apartment there.

All of Cindy's previous doubts about living away from home seemed to have disappeared. A bit too fast, I thought, and a bit too contingent on Joyce's suggestions. "I'm a little confused," I commented to Joyce. "Why are you giving Cindy so much advice? I can't tell if she really wanted to live in Hoboken, for example, or if she felt she had to follow your ideas."

"I don't think I told her what to do," Joyce said. "She wanted an apartment, so we talked about it, that's all."

I pointed out that a therapist has to be wary of presenting a patient like Cindy with what seems to be an agenda. It's all too easy for such a patient to switch one set of dependencies for another—from parents to therapist, for example—rather than seek a long-term solution to being dependent. It sounded to me as if Cindy, for all her new behavior, might be doing just that.

Also, I could not help wondering how those overprotective parents, the Morrisons, were reacting to the drastic changes in Cindy. According to Joyce, they were far from happy, although they were subsidizing both the apartment and the therapy. Basically, the Morrisons were maintaining a hands-off attitude. Joyce was surprised, because she had expected them to interfere with the therapy. The only explanation was that they had consulted a therapist of their own and were trying, as advised, to be more detached.

That detachment might soon be sorely tested, Joyce said, because Cindy had taken another big step. She had found a boyfriend, but he was not the type of boyfriend the Morrisons would want to write up in an engagement announcement. Marty Brun was a Hasidic Jew from Borough Park in Brooklyn. Cindy had met him at the manufacturing firm when he came to visit a cousin, one of the accountants.

Cindy's quest for independence, in the form of rebellion against her parents, had taken an interesting turn. Although I knew it wasn't funny, the picture of the tiny, blond WASP woman and the Orthodox Jewish young man, with his *payess* (earlocks) and black hat, teaming up to thumb their noses at their respective communities brought a smile to my face. I remembered my own rebellious activities as an adolescent, but they were mild enough compared to this.

"It must be terrifying for Cindy to separate from her infantalizing family," I commented to Joyce. "She's doing it with such a vengeance. She's got to feel desperate about being swallowed up by them, yet dependent on them at the same time. To get away, she's chosen two 'helpers' who are nothing at all like them—you and Marty." I told Joyce the relationship with Marty could be a positive step, but it wouldn't be easy. From what I knew of Cindy's history, she might have bitten off more than she could chew.

Joyce looked at me with extreme interest. Marty was the reason she had come, she reminded me. Cindy said she loved him, yet she was terrified of sleeping with him. And Marty was pressing her for a sexual relationship.

"I can't get her to deal with her own sexuality," Joyce said. She says she wants to have sex with Marty, yet she can't. But just as soon as she's decided she can't, she's back to thinking she can. She constantly shifts back and forth."

I wasn't surprised that sex with Marty was a major issue for Cindy. Identifying with a black woman, Joyce, had allowed her to become more independent. It had also allowed her sexuality to surface, since she also probably associated greater sexuality with black women. But sleeping with Marty would most certainly bring her into conflict with her moral values and jeopardize her relationship with her family.

Cindy said she wanted to break away from the Morrisons, but she undoubtedly continued to need their esteem. She might fear that an affair with Marty would alienate them, or cause some extreme behavior on her father's part. I thought about the way he had summarily removed Cindy from the University of Delaware when he learned her roommate was pregnant. What might he do if he thought Cindy was sexually active?

With all of these points to consider, I wondered why Joyce was in such a rush to have Cindy make a decision about sleeping with Marty. "Are we on some kind of timetable here?" I asked. "We don't have to set the world's record for achieving independence. Why don't you just sit back and let Cindy proceed at her own pace? It will be good for her to develop her own strength, rather than borrowing yours, which she seems to be doing a bit too much."

Joyce started slightly, making me think that time might indeed be an issue with her. Perhaps she worried that the Morrisons would somehow put a stop to the therapy. But as soon as she thought over what I had said, she relaxed. She would try to go slower, she remarked, as our session drew to a close.

Joyce told me she was going to be late for the "cocktail sip" she had mentioned when she came in. She was meeting her current boyfriend there, she confided. She had been dating Arnold, a successful free-lance photographer, for several months. "I'm beginning to think he's the one who won't move on," she said. "But, of course, I've hoped that before. Sometimes there seems to be a sign on my door that says '24-hour Parking Only.' "

She sounded a bit depressed, but she perked up as she checked her outfit and slipped some bracelets over her arm. "Sorry for the 'po' li'l me' routine," Joyce said with a smile as she walked out the door. "And by the way, I'm really glad I hooked up with you."

Watching her leave, I reflected that her independence might be burdensome as well as rewarding. I had heard many black professional women complain about the difficulty of finding—and keeping—a black man of compatible educational status and background. But I suspected, somehow, that

Joyce was talking about an internal conflict of her own, rather than a shortage of eligible men.

Over the next few weeks, as I got to know her better, she told me she had difficulty in getting close to men. The problem, she thought, could relate to the fact that her father had left the family when she was quite young. She had had some therapy of her own, she said, but it was brief. The therapist was a white woman, whom Joyce described as a "cold fish." Finally, she got tired of trying to talk to her and stopped the therapy. "She didn't seem to hear me," Joyce complained.

"Did you have any idea that racial differences might be part of the difficulty?" I asked, trying to get Joyce to acknowledge some of her feelings about white people.

She reflected for a moment. "I don't think race was a factor," she replied carefully. "In fact, except for her skin color, that therapist reminded me of Mama, never listening to what I said. Looking like she had a hot poker up her ass. Probably that's why I dropped her."

I felt it was important to press the issue. "Joyce," I said. "You were ready to acknowledge that Cindy chose you because you were black. Why did you choose a white therapist?"

"I think I was looking for someone different from my mother," she replied. "But ironically, she turned out to be a carbon copy. And if you're wondering why I came to you, maybe it's because you have a reputation for being a warm person."

So Joyce thought of white people as warmer, more sympathetic than blacks. Because of her experience with her mother, she associated blacks with emotional withdrawal. I didn't pursue this further, since it would be all too easy for a black supervisee or patient to perceive such pushing as sadistic or racist. It was best to wait and hope that insights would develop out of the supervision. As for Joyce's treatment of Cindy, during the weeks after our first session, she had tried to be more patient in her listening and less directive in what she said. She was anxious, however, because Cindy still didn't seem to be making any progress with Marty.

"I know," I said. "Sitting back and waiting can be hard. It takes a lot of skill."

Joyce smiled. "Sitting-on-the-duff type of skill, you mean," she said.

I assured her that some type of resolution would occur over time.

Despite her doubts about Cindy, Joyce was at what she called "a good time for me personally." Arnold had moved in with her, and although she didn't discuss the relationship in any detail, she was quite happy. That happiness, she said, was evidenced "by the colors I wear so much, orange and brown. They're my favorites. But, brother, if you ever see me in blue, boo hoo. All my friends know to get out of my way then."

"I'll remember that," I commented, wondering if I would ever experience a blue Joyce, or indeed, a nonvirginal Cindy.

I didn't have long to wait on the latter count. By my next session with Joyce, Cindy's reservations about sleeping with Marty had been resolved, swept away, in fact, by the events of a very rough day. Joyce described what had happened that day, as Cindy had described it to her. The day had started with Cindy on the telephone at work, holding off a bevy of angry suppliers wanting their checks. The manufacturing firm was in financial difficulty, a fact which heightened the usual tension and caused tempers to fray.

After she finished taking abuse from the suppliers, Cindy went on to hunt for an important order that was missing. She was not the person who had lost it, but she was the one the boss yelled at. His voice carried through the whole place. It seemed to Cindy that everyone was looking at her, blaming her for making the financial situation even more precarious.

As the rotten day drew to a close, there was a last straw. A buyer from the Midwest showed up unexpectedly, asking to see the new sportswear line, a collection of particularly skimpy shorts and tank tops. Since the regular model had left, Cindy was pressed into service. The buyer looked at the line with interest, and placed an order, which produced good feelings all around. But after everyone else had left the room, he cornered Cindy, putting his hand provocatively on her bare arm. Couldn't he take her out for a drink? He was sure she would enjoy his company.

Cindy ducked away and walked hastily down the hall. By the time she reached the front office, it was empty. Through the glass partition that separated the office from the workroom, she could see that only a few stockboys remained, and they were far in the back. The buyer followed her into the office and repeated his offer of a drink. Walking toward her, he looked like a monster from the fairy-tale books her father used to read to her years ago.

"Please don't," she said, as he moved close enough to warm her face with his breath. Cindy felt herself becoming flushed; her feet seemed to be cemented into the floor. With some effort, she pulled herself away from the buyer, picked up a pile of orders from the desk, and threw them in his face. Then she walked quickly out of the office, down the stairs, and out onto the street. Her heart was pounding, and her first thought was to telephone Joyce.

Joyce was with another patient and had little time to talk. She said she could arrange to see Cindy later that evening, in about two hours or so.

"I can't wait," Cindy cried.

She hung up the phone and called Marty, who appeared almost immediately. Cindy was waiting for him in a coffee shop near the office. He tried to calm her down, and finally he bundled her into his car and drove to Hoboken.

Having sex with Marty suddenly seemed like the most natural thing in the world. Although Cindy could not acknowledge it, she had been sexually aroused by the buyer. Now she directed those feelings toward Marty. She clung to him in desperation coupled with desire.

The sexual act itself was awkward. Marty didn't have much more experience than Cindy, but he was caring enough. She felt pleasure in his kisses, pain at penetration, and both closeness and anxiety when it was all over. In spite of her "scary feelings," Cindy told Joyce, she was glad she had gone to bed with Marty.

As she described these events to me, Joyce seemed to be reveling in them. Part of her agenda, I sensed, had been accomplished. "You were right, Wayne," she said with some satisfaction. "It seems as if things do work out by themselves, sometimes."

I was not as sanguine as Joyce. I told her that in my view, Cindy's losing her virginity wasn't necessarily all that wonderful. There was a lot of anxiety attached to it, and Joyce wasn't tuning in to that. She hadn't addressed the incident with the buyer, either, which Cindy clearly saw as traumatic. In effect, she was overlooking her patient's fears while applauding her "progress."

Joyce looked crestfallen. Perhaps she hadn't been sufficiently "on the ball," she acknowleged.

Joyce's own personal life wasn't going too well, I knew. She had not provided any details beyond the fact that she and Arnold were "getting into hassles," almost on the heels of his having moved in. I wondered what they were hassling over, but I was not Joyce's therapist. I suspected, however, that she could use one. For all of the men who had come and gone in her life, and her wide network of girlfriends, Joyce remained a very lonely woman.

She canceled our next two sessions, pleading an attack of the flu. Her voice sounded weary, which fit the symptoms well enough, but could also have signaled a dejected mood. I had a feeling that Arnold was no longer on the premises.

The next time I saw Joyce, her appearance was greatly subdued. Gone were the bright colors, gold jewelry, and effective makeup. She had wrapped a black scarf around her head rather than do her hair, and it gave the impression that she was grieving.

"I've had a rough two weeks, Wayne," she said.

"I expected to find you wearing blue," I commented.

Joyce laughed a bit uncomfortably. "He's not worth wearing

blue for," she said. "Arnold's really only small-time stuff. He walked out. Nothing new about that. So why are my ulcers giving me such a big-time pain in the gut?"

It was the first time she had mentioned having ulcers, and she was clearly in disabling pain.

"Do you have some medication?" I asked.

Joyce shook her head. "I'm better now," she said uncertainly, addressing her words to the floor.

"Let's talk about what happened," I suggested gently.

Joyce took a deep breath. Arnold, she told me, had come and gone like so many others. Each time Joyce had felt, here is a man I can trust. But each time, her trust was betrayed, usually when the man went off with another woman.

She was not aware of holding on too tight, of stifling her lovers, or of being unresponsive to them, but somehow she was doing something that drove them away. Her need for them was clearly too desperate. She was sure it had to do with the loss of her father, who had gone off with an old girlfriend of his. Her mother never mentioned her father's name again, and she didn't allow Joyce to mention it either.

She had only one thing to remind her of her father. It was a white dollhouse, which he had picked up in a state of disrepair on his rounds as a sanitation worker. The dollhouse had been thrown out by "one of the richest white families in town," Joyce told me. Her father had repainted the dollhouse, its furniture, and its inhabitants: a mother, father, son, and daughter—all of them shiny and white. Joyce loved to play with the dollhouse and the doll family. Here, everyone was safe and happy. The family had lots of things Joyce's family lacked. Fancy furniture for one thing. The dollhouse even had a chandelier, and the little girl doll's room had a tiny bed with four posters.

After her father abandoned the family, Joyce got even more attached to the dollhouse. Every morning she checked the dollhouse family to make sure they were all still there—and they were, including the father. That wasn't the way it was in real life, she knew. Her mama got a new boyfriend, "Uncle

Bill," but after a while, he left, too. But this time, Mama didn't seem to be too upset. She said that women had to learn to manage on their own. Mama had a whole bunch of sisters to help her, but Joyce had no one, especially since Mama paid less and less attention to her.

"What happened to the dollhouse?" I asked.

"It—it broke," Joyce said slowly, as if she didn't quite remember.

Recounting this story seemed to bring Joyce some relief. For a while we both sat there, sharing the silence. Finally, Joyce got up and went to the bathroom. When she came back, the black scarf was gone and makeup had been freshly applied. "Why didn't you tell me I was looking so mean, Wayne?" she asked. "Your mirror practically shouted at me, 'Get yourself together, girl.' "

We both laughed.

"Good advice," I commented gently. "But you know it can't be done with mirrors, Joyce. You should go back into therapy."

She nodded. She was thinking about doing just that. But this time, she wanted to be sure to pick the "right therapist."

After she left, I thought that Joyce, in addition to telling me very personal things, had also revealed additional attitudes toward white people. Not only did she see them as warm, she also viewed the white family as privileged, protected—and intact. What could this mean to her relationship with Cindy, who came from a "Dick and Jane" house, very much like Joyce's dollhouse? In Joyce's mind, the dollhouse was a good place to be. Yet she had seemed very intent on pushing Cindy out of it. Of course, she was helping Cindy to realize her own goals. Or was she? I suspected that the dollhouse was not only the object of Joyce's childhood fantasies but also of a countertransference dream that could jeopardize Cindy.

Over the next few weeks, I felt compelled to step up pressure to understand the countertransference problem, because Joyce told me that Cindy was showing evidence of being increasingly troubled. The major symptom was a moderate depression—listlessness and lack of interest in anything. Joyce said she felt responsible, at least in part. She had canceled her appointments with Cindy while she was going through her own emotional turmoil. Now she worried that she had behaved unprofessionally, and I could not convince her that she had not. "There's no benefit in feeling guilty," I said. "Why did Cindy say she was depressed?"

At their last session, Cindy had insisted there was "no reason." Yet Joyce knew of at least two: the clothing manufacturing firm was going under, and Marty was pressing Cindy hard to move in with him. These factors had apparently created great pressure and Cindy mentioned that she was thinking about going home. She wanted to get away from everything.

Joyce had warned that Cindy might regret not "sticking it out." Adults solved their problems rather than running away from them, she commented. I couldn't help thinking that it was a case of "Do as I say, not as I do," an attitude not uncommon among therapists.

The night after that warning, Cindy told Joyce that she had had a dream. She was in a limousine, being driven toward New York City at breakneck speed. The chauffeur seemed to be out of control, eventually taking a wrong turn, and they ended up, Cindy thought, in Newark, Delaware, where the University of Delaware is located. But the university buildings looked quite strange. Some were partially burned out, and in others the windows were boarded up. There was a riot going on. Some angry students were throwing Molotov cocktails from the rooftops. Other students surrounded the limousine and banged on the windows, asking Cindy if she was available for sex. All of a sudden, one of the Molotovs blew up near the car. There was a terrific explosion and Cindy woke up in the early morning, shaking. The first thing she did was to call her parents, "Just to see how they were doing."

When Joyce and Cindy discussed Cindy's associations to the dream, it seemed it might reflect a lingering desire to return to the University of Delaware. Upon returning, however,

Cindy realized that the university was not at all the way she remembered it. It had become, instead, a dangerous place. In Joyce's view, this meant that Cindy wanted to continue on to New York City and return to some sort of job.

This interpretation struck me as completely off-base. In the dream, Cindy expressed no desire to get back to New York. And why should the University of Delaware have become so threatening? I thought Joyce was suppressing the true meaning of the dream, and I asked her whether she had asked Cindy the color of the chauffeur in the dream or the color of the rioters.

Joyce looked at me hard. "What are you getting at, Wayne?" she said.

"Just the fact that you're being color-blind to the way Cindy sees you," I commented. "You only want to understand the positive side of her feelings about blacks, but in this dream, she's come up with a lot of negatives."

In the dream, I postulated, Joyce was the chauffeur, driving Cindy and the treatment at breakneck speed into New York City. The place they diverted to was most likely Newark, New Jersey, which is more associated with riots and burned-out buildings than Newark, Delaware. Newark, New Jersey, has a large black population. I was willing to bet that the angry rioters who tossed the Molotovs and solicited Cindy were black, and that the chauffeur who drove Cindy into sexual and physical danger was also black. The limousine was probably black, too.

"Don't you think that Cindy's terror reflects the feeling that you and Marty—who has got to be linked with you in her mind —pushed her too fast toward separation and sexuality?" I asked. "She must be angry at you, too, about her job blowing up in her face. Now all that rebelliousness you unleashed toward her family has 'blacklashed' on to you. It's the negative side of the transference. You've become the crazy chauffeur, the whorey therapist, and the urban terrorist, all wrapped up into one messy package. She's certainly displacing her anger onto something black," I concluded.

"Oh, shit!" Joyce said.

"There you go, doing the same thing," I joked, hoping to break the tension.

Joyce laughed. "No, shit is brown," she observed, "but black is shittier. It's like the old poem says: 'If you're black, stand back./If you're brown, hang around./If you're white, you're all right.' "

I wondered where Joyce thought she fit into this verse.

"Black enough to stand back, friend, can't you see that?" she exclaimed bitterly. She held her arm up to the light so that I could observe its dark color. Then she went on to say she was the same color as her mother, while the woman her father had left her mother for was light-skinned.

Joyce said that she had believed her father had gone away because she and her mother were too dark. "I used to scrub myself over and over in the tub, trying to get lighter, so he'd come back. I even bought 'lightening cream' with some of the food money. Mama had a fit. She said I was crazy, and she hid the cream. But I kept on trying to get some. It was one of the things we used to argue about, until we stopped talking altogether."

Even though that time was long past, the sadness remained. Joyce associated her own color not only with independence and strength, but with rejection and pain. Like Cindy, she attached several negative feelings to the color black. It was something I had observed happening quite frequently in the dreams of both black and white patients. Out-of-control sexual and aggressive feelings, for example, are often connected to a black figure, while the figures who are in control of their sexuality and aggression are usually white. The fact that both races dream this way shows how deeply the biases of our society affect our psyches.

The colors black and white, I found in studies I have performed, figure prominently in the dreams of black patients twice as often as they do in the dreams of white patients. I think this means that in sleep, the black dreamer re-creates the mine field of his or her waking life, with its unending round of terrifying interactions with whites. In dreams, black patients try to undo the daily ignominy, just as soldiers suffering from post-traumatic stress syndrome relive their combat agonies in the hope of ending them.

Joyce had heard me discuss all this in the lecture on interracial therapy that had caused her to seek me out. But she had trouble dealing with the notion that sweet little Cindy associated so many negative qualities with her favorite role model, black Joyce. She had the guts, however, to raise the issue with Cindy at their next session. Yes, Cindy admitted shamefacedly, every last person in the dream was black, with the possible exception of one of the students banging on the window of the limousine. But he was dressed all in black. She thought it might have been Marty.

The dream had terrified Cindy. But now, as she and Joyce discussed it, she realized it also allowed her to release her anger, rather than submerge it in depression. Her relationship with Marty had become frightening to her, she said, as he pressured her to move in with him and to "do more" in bed. He apparently saw her as the stereotypical *shiksa*—the Yiddish word for an unmarried gentile woman—and he expected her to be more sexually expressive than he thought Jewish women were. After all, she had agreed to go to bed with him without being married, something that he imagined a woman of his own Orthodox religious group would be unlikely to do. Cindy had been using Marty in her rebellion, but he was using her, too.

As the result of Marty's pressure, Cindy's long-standing sexual guilts had surfaced, and she felt like a whore. She made that clear—and punished herself—by having the "students" in the dream solicit her. And now she blamed Joyce for her feelings of shame. She felt it was Joyce who had given her permission to sleep with Marty.

"Hey, wait a minute, when did I say that?" Joyce had asked. She was stunned to learn how much Cindy had been hanging on her every word, searching pathetically for the direction in which she should go. Apparently my suggestion that Cindy had exchanged her dependence on her parents for dependence on her therapist was valid.

Now Cindy seemed ready to reverse the process. She told Joyce that going back home to live, at least for a while, might be a good idea. When she had called her parents after the dream, they were cordial, and Cindy realized how much she wanted to be with them. Yet she felt she was betraying Joyce. The session ended with Cindy in tears.

The next afternoon, when Joyce told me all of this, she was wearing a blue dress. I knew she associated the color with extreme distress. Was she upset because she feared the therapy had failed?

Joyce shook her head no. In fact, her state of equanimity surprised her. That morning, she said, she had felt compelled to put on the dress, as she usually did when things were totally crummy. But in the course of the day, her mood had changed. Strangely, she had started to feel quite good. In fact, she had lightened up considerably.

"Without any cream?" I commented.

"What?" Joyce asked.

"You got lighter without any cream," I repeated, "maybe because Cindy is going back with the light-skinned people, where it's safe and warm."

I expected Joyce to get angry, to fight the idea, but she didn't. Her own emotions reflected the truth of what I was saying. She couldn't help noticing the relief she was experiencing as the treatment collapsed, and Cindy, "the doll," decided to return to the white dollhouse.

Joyce was at last ready to shine a "light" on her countertransference problem. I told her I thought things might fit together this way. Subconsciously, she viewed the Morrisons as protective, caring, and emotionally close, while ignoring their overbearing and dangerously infantalizing aspects. Most important to Joyce, the Morrison family was intact. There was a strong father on the scene, and he wanted to take care of his little girl, as Joyce herself had always wanted to be taken care of.

For Joyce, the positive qualities of the Morrisons were a function of their whiteness. In her fantasy, she believed her father would have stayed around had she been whiter, and they would have been happy in the dollhouse. Like many children who feel helpless, Joyce blamed herself for her father's leaving, and she attached the guilt to her skin color. When she took on Cindy as a patient, she consciously wanted to serve as a role model for a young woman whose growth toward independence was severely retarded. But unconsciously, she envied Cindy the luxury of being dependent. Joyce's own dependency needs had never been adequately met.

By pushing Cindy to separate prematurely, by encouraging her "rebellious" romance with a lover who could only prove extremely problematic, and by ignoring Cindy's severe anxieties, Joyce could make sure that her patient's attempt at independence would fail. Her withdrawal of support, in the form of canceling several appointments during a traumatic period for Cindy, had added to the "push." The end result was that Cindy was subverted back to the dollhouse, where Joyce subconsciously thought she belonged, and where Joyce herself ached to be. This was confirmed by a remark, almost a confession, that Joyce now made about the Morrisons. "They dote on Cindy so, and they're all together—and they mean to keep it that way." There was a tone of longing in her voice.

Joyce reacted to my analysis like someone who sees the pieces of a distant puzzle coming together. They fit, but the picture needs to be closer to be fully comprehended. That would take time. To my mind, the puzzle wasn't totally complete either. Joyce's feelings about the Morrisons were so intense, I thought there might be more to the dollhouse fantasy than we had yet discussed. Her countertransference dream had a reparative quality to it, a putting back together. How did the real dollhouse get broken? And what about the blue dress? Did she wear it simply to "sing the blues"? I doubted it.

Facing these questions, my instinct told me, was going to be the tough part for Joyce. I was right. When I said, "Tell me about the blue dress, Joyce," her stomach pains erupted with a vengeance. This time the agony was so severe she could hardly speak.

I was ready to drop the subject, when she waved her hand at me. "I want to discuss it, Wayne, I really do," she said, barely managing to gasp out the words. I got her a glass of water and waited until her voice returned.

The trauma had occurred on a spring day when she was eleven years old, Joyce began. She had returned from school to find nobody home. That was not unusual, since Mama was working. Joyce was used to taking care of things. She cleaned up the kitchen and hung out a pile of wet wash. Then she settled down to play with her dollhouse.

She was totally absorbed in her game, when she heard footsteps behind her. They belonged to "Uncle Bill," her mother's boyfriend. Joyce liked Uncle Bill, and he made Mama happier than she had been for a long time. He sat down beside her, and they chatted about the dollhouse family, as they frequently did. But today was different. Uncle Bill looked at her oddly and drew her up on his lap. Suddenly, she could feel his hand reaching beneath her panties, touching her in a place she knew was private. He rubbed his hand back and forth and Joyce felt flustered and frightened. There was something wrong about this, she knew. She tried to break away, but Uncle Bill wouldn't let her go.

Instead, he picked her up and carried her into the back bedroom. There, on a bed covered with a blue cotton bedspread, he removed her clothing. The color blue was emblazoned in her memory, the way the material pressed against her skin, swallowing her up and drowning her. Joyce was senseless with fear, then pain, as he forced himself on her.

Before he left, Uncle Bill warned her not to tell her mama. This would be just their secret, he said. As Joyce suspected, she had done something terrible, just as she must have done something terrible to make Daddy leave. The white dollhouse was no good. It would never bring Daddy back now. She went into the kitchen and got out the rolling pin Mama used to make biscuits. Then she struck hard at the dollhouse, totally splintering it and breaking the doll family into little pieces.

When Mama came home, the remains of the dollhouse were sticking out of the garbage pail. "What did you go and do that for?" she asked.

"I got tired of it," Joyce replied, fighting back tears.

Her mother looked at her strangely. Somehow, Joyce knew, she suspected something. From that day on, there was a distance between them, and within a day or so, Uncle Bill had gone. From that time, too, Joyce always wore blue after something bad happened.

Joyce was shaking as she finished speaking, and she clutched at the neckline of her blue dress. She had never told anyone about the rape before. No wonder the idea of protection was so important to her. Her father, by leaving, and her mother, by being at work, had failed to protect her from Uncle Bill. The white dollhouse fantasy had fallen apart, but with Cindy's return to the Morrisons, the dollhouse would regain its strength, and the little girl inside Joyce could renew her hope of being healed.

Such healing, Joyce knew now, could only come through therapy of her own. When she asked me for a recommendation, I suggested a black male therapist who was extremely supportive and warm. It would be good for Joyce to see that a black male could have these qualities and share them with her. That would certainly contribute to a readjustment of her stereotypes about black men and blackness generally.

Just as Joyce had displaced everything unsafe onto black families, she idealized a "dollhouse" white family like the Morrisons. Yet, I commented, white families were far from perfect, and many were far from safe. The Morrisons' extreme need to keep Cindy from growing up indicated a pathology of some sort. They were hiding something of their own, perhaps a dysfunctional relationship between husband and wife that made them empty without their daughter.

It would be best, I thought, if Cindy didn't go back home to be swallowed up once more. If she did, she might never break free again. I suggested that Joyce tell Cindy she would be failing herself if she returned home. If she heeded that statement and remained in treatment with Joyce, Joyce could pursue a middle course with her, one that would allow Cindy to separate in her own time and within the limits of her fears. Cindy might be more secure living with a roommate, for example, or in a group environment. Perhaps she could look for a job that was more structured and less stressful.

"There's a gray area, you know, between black and white," I said.

Joyce smiled weakly. It would take a long time, I knew, before she really felt like smiling.

Joyce continued to treat Cindy for several years. In the course of the treatment, Cindy went back to school in New York City and got a degree in early childhood education. Eventually, she took a teaching job out of town, completing a separation not only from her parents, but from Joyce as well.

Joyce's own therapy went on for a long time, too, but it went well. The last time I spoke to her was on the telephone. She had realized, she said, that her dream wasn't really of being white, but of having the advantages white people had. A lot of those advantages were real enough, but others were fantasies of Joyce's own making. There is no safe white dollhouse, she had learned, for any of us.

The reason for Joyce's call was to tell me about a real dream, a "good-bye dream" that involved me. She was lying on the ground, rather like Sleeping Beauty, when I appeared in the guise of a fairy-tale prince and kissed her sweetly on the lips, waking her up.

"Don't worry, Wayne," Joyce said. "It was a fatherly kiss. Of course, you were standing in for my father in the dream— and in real life, you were the one who wakened me to what was going on. But there's one more detail about the dream I want you to know."

"What's that?" I asked.

"In it, you were black."

CHAPTER 4

The Dream of Envy

Envy is one of the most universal of human feelings. And it's one of the most difficult for us to acknowledge in ourselves. But when a therapist yearns after what patients have, he can be driven to violate the canons of the profession. He can victimize his patients and, in turn, be victimized by them. It's a strange collusion, and one of which the colluding parties are usually unaware. That doesn't make it less dangerous, though. Just the opposite.

When Leonard first phoned to ask me to supervise him, I had little reason to suspect him of any ulterior motives. He sounded forthright enough. He had heard, he said, that I had an important practice and that I sometimes supervised other therapists who needed help with a particular case. He wasn't having difficulty with a specific patient, yet he felt he needed the "added insight" supervision would provide. "Sometimes I really screw up," he said disarmingly. I thought that I was going to like him.

At our first meeting, I was struck by Leonard's commanding presence. In his early thirties, he was tall and athletically built, with thick black hair and rough-hewn features. His imposing frame seemed to fill the entire doorway. But a quick smile softened the sharp angles of his face and made him look more human.

"I'm really looking forward to working with you," he said, as he clasped my hand warmly. His dark eyes lingered on my face for a moment, as if to establish intimacy. Then he strode confidently into the room.

He was attired expensively and impeccably, but he seemed to be dressed for the boardroom rather than the consulting room. Instead of the rumpled tweedy look affected by many analysts, he wore a blue pin-striped suit, white shirt, striped silk tie, and highly polished black shoes with black socks. This corporate image was belied, however, by an open, almost boyish charm.

Leonard looked around with interest at the pictures I have on my office walls of animals taken on an African photo safari, and remarked that he, too, was interested in photography. He had a photograph collection of his own, he told me, mainly of sports activities, like football and basketball. He confided that he was really "into sports," and not only as a spectator. He was a "compulsive" squash player and didn't miss a day at one of New York's top racquet clubs, although his time was always highly scheduled and his practice quite busy.

As if to drive home the point, he glanced at his watch. Then, perhaps fearful of having impressed me as being overly driven, he settled back in his chair and stretched out his long legs. But even in this determinedly relaxed state, energy seemed to be emanating from his pores. His gaze was intense as he waited for me to take over the conversation.

The first stage of supervision is always exciting, yet tricky. Like most therapists, I'm a curious individual, or I wouldn't have been attracted to the profession. Supervising gives me the chance to find out about several unique people at once: the therapist and his patients. What are the problems? What's going wrong with the treatment?

My curiosity is more easily satisfied than it is in the therapeutic relationship. I find out things about patients without having to probe. What's more, I don't have to take responsibility for the outcomes of the therapy. But on the other hand, I have to tread lightly in scrutinizing the therapeutic relationships of my supervisees. My goal is to share my expertise without taking over.

As I do with every new supervisee, I began by asking Leonard to tell me something about his background and his education. He told me that he came from California and had grown up in a large Italian-American family. His immigrant grandfather was a successful tomato grower, but Leonard's father had greatly expanded the family fortunes by opening several canning factories.

Leonard described his family as close-knit and boisterous, "a bunch of *paesano* Kennedys." Yet nowadays, he said, he rarely saw his siblings. "Truth to tell, Wayne," he said lightly, "I'm the black sheep in the family." His brothers were all successful entrepreneurs and one sister has married a multimillionaire. So Leonard's income was small potatoes to his family, even though it was quite substantial for a young psychiatrist.

The size of Leonard's fees, which he made a point of telling me, were my first clue to his avarice. "My patients can afford to pay," he said, perhaps in response to the surprised expression on my face. "They're mainly successful lawyers, accountants, and businesspeople, just like your patients."

"How do you know about my patients?"

"Well, I just assumed," he said mildly, and smiled at me.

Leonard quickly shifted the subject to his education. He had gone to a prestigious western medical school and then come to New York for training at one of the better psychiatric institutes. Although his training had been excellent in many respects, Leonard said his technique needed "strengthening." "Sometimes it seems to take me forever to figure out what's wrong," he said. "That's where I want help."

Whether or not it took "forever," Leonard seemed to have a good enough handle on the reasons for his patients' problems, as I found out when I asked him to talk about his current cases. Not only were his insights sound, I was struck by the amount of empathy and concern he demonstrated when he described his patients. The craggy structure of his face seemed to soften, and his voice took on a compelling tone. He told me how he had canceled a vacation to accommodate the worsening depression of one patient, rather than risk having the man adjust to being treated by a covering psychiatrist.

The patient was one of his "specialties," he said, a professional with a cocaine habit. For these people, he often made himself available around the clock because "when they need you, they need you." When he took on a patient, he said, he was absolutely committed to spending all the time needed to help the person get better.

While Leonard's energy and dedication were laudable, he had another quality that wasn't quite as attractive. When he spoke about his patients, he provided an inordinate amount of detail about the material side of their lives. In fact, a large part of his enthusiasm seemed to be reserved for these details. He told me that one patient, a television executive, dined at Le Cirque at least three times a week and regularly flew to London on the Concorde. Recently, this man had attended a party at which an Academy Award winner was the guest of honor. Nor had the actress been the only celebrity present. Leonard reeled off the names of the others, what they had been wearing, and what type of caviar had been served. He ended the recitation by detailing the executive's yearly salary and his stock options. The figures seemed to make him gloomy, and he glanced down at his highly polished shoes, as if to seek inspiration. "We're in the wrong business, Wayne," he murmured.

Now it's not unusual for a therapist to be aware of—or even gratified by—a patient's wealth and status; what's unusual is to pay so much attention to them, to be so goddamned impressed. And the amount of information Leonard knew about his patients indicated to me that he had pressed them for unnecessary details. A patient may mention going to a party and even who was there, but he doesn't normally repeat the menu, unless he's a restaurant critic or a caterer. Clearly Leonard needed this type of information. It made him feel good and bad at the same time. What a curious blend of altruism and envy he is, I thought. It promised to be an interesting supervisory experience.

The next few weeks, however, were anything but interesting. Leonard arrived at our meetings in his usual state of energy, but when I asked him how things were going, his general answer was a bland "fine." Sometimes therapists sit back too far and let clues go by, hesitant to probe too much. Leonard's bland reports indicated that he was challenging his patients too little.

The television executive, for example, regularly took out his work problems on his family. Arriving home one evening after a particularly stressful day, he tripped over his nine-year-old's bike in the driveway. He picked up the offending vehicle and hurled it against the garage door wall, twisting the wheels entirely out of commission. He followed that by dressing down his son in front of the neighborhood kids, who had gathered to see what the noise was about. Leonard's only comment on this story had been to remark to his patient that he "must have been under considerable tension."

The executive's behavior toward his wife contained similar elements of abuse. He put her down at every opportunity, yet Leonard failed to point this out. "Why do you think you're steering clear of this subject?" I asked him.

"Well, Wayne, the guy's boss is on his back over this deal with the Coast. As soon as it gets worked out, I'm sure he'll calm down."

"It sounds to me as if he's very angry. How come you're not addressing his rage?"

Leonard once again murmured something about pressure. He was rationalizing the problem, pushing it under the rug. Therapists want to be liked, too, and sometimes they'll fail to raise a particular issue for fear of antagonizing the patient, of driving him or her away. That's what I suspected was happening with Leonard.

His behavior left me with no doubt that Leonard had a lot invested emotionally in his relationships with his patients. Vicariously, he lived their social lives and acquired their status symbols. He wanted that kind of life, and he wanted what they had. In the case of the television executive, Leonard preferred to overlook his violence and comment on his financial expertise. The "deal" with the Coast, Leonard told me, would bring in another $40 million for the network, and big bonuses for the executive. Part of the bonus money was already allocated for a beach home in Jamaica, which he proceeded to describe to me. I scarcely listened. I was annoyed with Leonard for deliberately sabotaging the point I was making, for shying away from a very troublesome aspect of his patient's personality.

A few weeks later, I had even more reason to be irritated. Our session took place the day after the annual Emmy Awards. Leonard was still agog with excitement. He and his wife, a fledgling actress, had attended the awards ceremony along with the television executive, who had given Leonard a pair of tickets.

As Leonard sat there looking at me with a pleased expression on his face, I could scarcely believe he had been trained at a major psychiatric institute. Every therapist is taught that it is an abuse of patient trust to have a social relationship with a patient. Such relationships take advantage of the patient's idealized feelings for the therapist. When I pointed this out, Leonard squirmed.

"Heck, Wayne, he just left the tickets on my desk. I didn't even talk to him at the awards. We were sitting at another table."

"Stop trying to con me, Leonard. Taking those tickets was a first step toward corruption. Whenever a patient does something like that, you've got to ask why. Usually, he or she is subconsciously out to seduce you in some fashion."

"I didn't think of it that way," Leonard responded.

Apparently, it was not the first time Leonard had allowed himself to step over the line. I learned that he had taken a number of "favors" from patients. Just a few months before he started supervision, he and his wife had gone to a house party in the Caribbean. The invitation came from a patient who was to be another one of the guests. In Leonard's eyes, the fact that the patient wasn't the host made it "all right." Here, too, he told me, he had scarcely seen the patient, but had spent all his time deep-sea fishing with the host and a group of other guests. There were plenty of "movers and shakers" at the party, he noted, and he hoped that some of them might refer patients to him or become patients themselves.

Leonard had occasionally dropped hints of his desire to "upgrade" his practice. It was a sub-rosa reason he was seeing me, I discovered, for he kept asking if I knew this or that internist and whether the doctor in question ever referred patients to me. He wanted a super-duper practice, even more super-duper than the one he had, and by introducing him to other specialists, I could be an important link in his referral network.

I didn't mind helping him, if I could—that's legitimate enough—but I hadn't realized he was "fishing" for patients in forbidden waters as well. What a user the guy is, I thought. How could I have ever found him charming?

Well, there was a certain charm in Leonard's very openness. Maybe he honestly didn't know he was doing something wrong. More likely, he knew and was conflicted about it. After all, he had brought up the Emmy Awards himself and then gone on to describe his other exploits. He was dragging them in by the back door, casually dropping them on my desk the same way the television executive had dropped the tickets. There was a good chance he was asking me for help in dealing with his covetousness.

Leonard's behavior saddened me as much as it made me angry, because I knew him to be a talented therapist. Yet he was sabotaging his own expertise.

During our first meeting I had found out that Leonard had undergone a year of therapy and that he had not seen a therapist for the past five years. Unfortunately, his training program had not required him to have substantial analysis. No training programs do, even though a therapist's own problems clearly affect the way he performs with his patients. I strongly suggested that Leonard go back into treatment. He said that he would think about it. Facing up to his countertransference problem would be difficult, I knew. After all, his envy had proved to be a valuable asset. It enabled him to go after—and achieve—many of the things he wanted.

I decided I would give him some time to think about it, then bring up the subject of treatment again. But it turned out that time was one thing we did not have. Just a few weeks previously, and unknown to me, Leonard had started treating a patient who would employ Leonard's envy to his own subconscious advantage.

The patient's name was Clayborne Rhodes, Leonard told me, when he finally decided to bring him up. "It's an old WASP name," he said. The case had been stumping him for several months, he added, but he had wanted to try to solve it on his own before consulting me. Being stumped was an extremely uncomfortable feeling for a person of Leonard's self-confidence.

All therapists encounter patients they find difficult to help. These patients play into blind spots, either positive or negative countertransference feelings. When a therapist is enamored of a patient, or wants something out of him or her, he won't put too much pressure on the patient to change. If a patient makes a therapist angry—because he or she reminds the therapist of a parent, for example—that patient may not be handled appropriately. Why, I wondered, was Leonard stumped?

I asked him to tell me about Clayborne Rhodes. He was, Leonard said, a Wall Street investment banker with Stanton Frank, a firm with a reputation for being involved in the hottest deals. This was at the beginning of the go-go eighties, and Wall Street was clearly the place for someone who valued success as measured by a rapid rise to power and big-figure returns.

It was not as if Clay needed the money, Leonard told me. His was an old-monied family, with roots going back to colonial New York, and with banking connections of almost as long standing. The typical path for Rhodes males was to attend a prep school—Groton usually—then Yale, perhaps a graduate business school, and then on to the brokerage house where Clay's father, Alden Rhodes, had succeeded his father who had succeeded his father, and so on back into the misty, regal past.

This long line of stalwart succession, however, had been broken by Clay. He found the family firm, Lanham & Ellis, too stodgy and moribund to interest him. In his view, there was no future there. Instead, he accepted an offer from Stanton Frank, where the "art of the deal" was practiced with precision, and within a few short years—Clay was only twenty-eight—he had achieved success beyond anything his family might have considered seemly. He commanded a high six-figure income with a large year-end bonus. He had acquired many of the yuppie accoutrements of the eighties: a Ferrari, a co-op apartment on Park Avenue, a summer home in the Hamptons not far from Leonard's own, and a taste for fine clothes, food, and wine.

Leonard's voice, as he described Clayborne Rhodes, showed that he had lost none of his enthusiasm for all the accoutrements of success. He commented that even his sister, the one who had married the multimillionaire, would be hard-pressed to match Clay's wealth. "And he's so damned young, too," he added.

The voice of envy, but also the voice of satisfaction. Leonard was delighted with the fact that Clay was the first Wall Streeter among his patients. Clay had, in fact, been referred by another banker Leonard had met on the Caribbean trip. So his unethical behavior had borne the fruit he desired. That, I realized, would diminish the effectiveness of my "moral blandishments." Still, Leonard continued to want my supervision, which meant he also wanted some direction toward the "straight and narrow." I didn't expect Leonard to lose his ambivalence. It was part of the challenge of supervising him.

"Why did Clay come to see you?" I asked.

"He's having anxiety attacks. They began when he started working at Stanton Frank, and they've grown worse. Suddenly, while sitting in a business meeting or at his desk, he's seized by a feeling of dread. His heart starts to race and his palms become sweaty. He feels as if he has to run out of the room, but he manages to restrain himself from doing that. His family practitioner gave him some tranquilizers. Truth to tell, they're doing more good than I am. I simply can't figure out what's behind the attacks."

Anxiety is one of the most common reasons that a person comes into treatment. It can be nearly crippling, as Clay's attacks were, or it can be more subtle. Still, the patient's life is severely affected. Like Clay, he may fear that he's going to fall apart. Anxiety attacks can appear out of the blue. The patient is fine until one day he's driving his car or standing on a supermarket line, and he gets a feeling of dread. His adrenaline soars, his heart starts to pound, and he fears he's going to die. The first attack is like a shock to the system. After that, a self-fulfilling cycle develops. The patient gets anxious just anticipating an attack, and the attacks begin to feed on themselves, until they are well entrenched.

When anxiety is the problem, I consider several possible causes: loss of or separation from a loved one; a threat to self-esteem, such as a confrontation with psychological overtones of castration; a loss of identity—the blurring of the boundaries between the individual and another person; and going against one's conscience. Of course, there can be more than one cause. And in some cases, anxiety seems to run in families.

Leonard had anticipated some of my questions. No, there was no family history of anxiety, he told me. Nor were there any family or sexual problems that he knew of. In fact, Clay's sleek Social Register fiancée and his prowess in bed with her were other items on the long list of things Leonard envied about him.

Although the office was the scene of the anxiety attacks, there didn't seem to be anything really wrong there either. I postulated that Clay might be in conflict with a superior who resembled his father or a sibling, but Leonard assured me this was not likely to be the case. "He doesn't have any brothers or sisters. And there's no similarity between the father and the boss. The father takes a gentlemanly, almost detached approach to making money, while the boss is a hard-driving hotshot. He thinks the sun rises and sets on Clay, and he lets Clay know it too. I'm fairly certain that Clay's sweaty palms have nothing to do with his job in mergers and acquisitions. He enjoys the feeling of being a high roller."

Leonard, I knew, liked the feeling too, especially when he could absorb it vicariously through Clay. Two birds of a feather, I thought, two hustlers at work.

Knowing that everything that happens on Wall Street was not necessarily squeaky clean, I asked whether there was anything about Clay's activities that could be causing a guilty conscience.

Leonard hesitated for a moment. "Well, he's done what he had to do to get ahead."

"Such as?"

"Such as hiring a call girl for a client he wanted to woo away from another firm."

"He told you about that?"

"Yes, and other things, too. He talks a lot about what's happening on the Street. If he hears about a takeover that may be coming up, or a new product being developed by some corporation, he'll mention it."

"What do you say when he tells you about call girls and things like that?"

I wasn't surprised when the answer turned out to be not much. Leonard was too in awe of being taken into Clay's confidence to risk losing the relationship by questioning his actions. His justification was that he needed to be nonjudgmental so that Clay would confide in him, and he could learn more about the reasons for the anxiety.

I pointed out that being nonjudgmental doesn't mean you leave issues unaddressed. "By not saying anything, he may think you approve," I commented. "Clay may really want you to come down harder on him. Perhaps that's why he's telling you some of this," I said, thinking of Leonard's own confidences to me.

"Perhaps," he replied mildly, playing the good supervisee.

A thought occurred to me. "What does old Alden Rhodes think of all this—the prostitute and whatever other little shortcuts Clay arranges?"

Leonard had no idea. But at a later session with Clay, when he talked about hiring a corporate spy to ferret out a rival firm's secrets, Leonard asked him, "What would your father say to that?"

"I don't mention it to him," Clay said. "He's much too old-fashioned for this sort of stuff. No wonder Stanton Frank is miles ahead of Lanham and Ellis."

Leonard wondered if Clay's bravado had something to do with his anxiety. He began to monitor his comments about his father extra carefully. "Clay becomes agitated when he talks about the old man," he told me at our next session. "Usually his voice is flat, with that kind of prep-school drawl, like when he mentions a new hotshot company that bears watching. But when the subject is his father, his words come out like machine-gun fire. Rat-a-tat-tat. Almost as if he was taking aim at the guy."

As I waited for Leonard to continue, I wondered why Clay told him about so many "hotshot" new companies. But I skipped over it, because I wanted to explore what Leonard was saying about Clay's tone of voice when he spoke of his father. Often voice tone is as important as what the patient tells us. It can be a tip-off to many things: hostility, love, depression—and sometimes all three.

According to Leonard, the anger in Clay's voice when he talked about his father seemed to be connected to the pot-shots that gentleman, previously described as so mild-mannered, constantly took at Stanton Frank. "They bend the rules so much, you wonder why they don't fall over backwards" was one such remark.

"He thinks he's so goddamned morally superior," Clay had sneered.

Clay also responded to Leonard's inquiries about his father by opening up and revealing some previously withheld information. Lanham & Ellis, the family firm, had been in financial trouble for a year. It could not keep up with the current climate. Even old WASP clients, longtime friends of Alden's, were switching to firms that were willing to "bend the rules."

"L and E has only itself to blame," Clay had blurted out. "They're dinosaurs over there. And Dad's the king of the dinosaurs, a tyrannosaurus."

"I thought it was an interesting analogy," Leonard told me. "Technically, nobody's to blame for the death of a dinosaur, even one who's a tyrant. But a king has to have a successor, usually his son. And the whole idea of succession can raise feelings of guilt, even if the dead king alone was responsible for his demise."

Leonard shuffled through some notes as he spoke. I could almost share the thought processes in his brain.

"You know," he said finally, "Clay's anxiety attacks started about a year ago, several months before he came to see me. That's about the same time Alden told him about the difficulties at L and E. It's also the same time that Clay's own career at Stanton Frank took off. So Clay not only has to wheel and deal, a physically and mentally exhausting activity even though he loves it, he also has to bury his guilt feelings about dear old Dad. It could be enough to make anyone's palms sweaty."

It was the beginning of a hypothesis. Clay's anxiety related to his feelings about surpassing Alden Rhodes. A son's doing better than his father is a situation that might invoke guilt, but doesn't necessarily do so. Many sons rise higher than their fathers without experiencing adverse psychological effects, particularly if their fathers are proud of them. But that didn't seem to be the case here.

Clay's symptoms indicated that he thought he was responsible for the demise of Alden Rhodes. But what would that demise mean to him? Did killing Dad off mean castrating him or taking Mom away from him, becoming king of the hill? Or did it mean that he was pursuing a forbidden path in sex or work? Since Clay reported no sexual difficulties, the forbidden path seemed to be related to work. Stanton Frank, for all its promise to Clay, was a place that Alden Rhodes had put off-limits. Yet it was here that Clay had dared to thrive, while Alden entered a decline.

But even Clay may not have suspected how swiftly that decline would proceed. Just a few days after my session with Leonard, Alden Rhodes arranged to have dinner with Clay. They poked away decorously at a dinner of roast beef and parslied potatoes at the Yale Club, during which little was said. Then, Alden dropped his bombshell over coffee. He had "stepped down," he said simply, from his position at Lanham & Ellis.

"Stepped down" was the way *The New York Times* put it, too, Clay reported to Leonard. The article went on to say that Alden had left "to pursue long-standing interests." "That's the way firms like that say he got the boot," Clay said. "They never wash their dirty linen in public, never get written up in *New York* magazine like Stanton Frank."

In spite of his sarcastic tone, Clay's basic reaction to Alden's forced departure was devastation. In fact, he had phoned and asked to see Leonard immediately. Leonard detailed what happened at that session.

Clay arrived in a distracted state, his mind almost as disheveled as his clothing. His impeccable Brooks Brothers suit, the same blue pinstripe Leonard was partial to, was wrinkled from shoulders to cuffs, almost as if he had slept in it. Gone was the prep-school drawl or even the staccato anger Leonard had noted at the previous session. In fact, after talking about his father, Clay burst into tears. "Real hard sobs" was the way Leonard described them.

Clay grabbed Kleenex after Kleenex out of a box on Leonard's lamp table. After a time, he regained his composure. He was, he said, utterly amazed at his reaction to "Dad's being canned." It wasn't as if he hadn't expected something to happen. Perhaps it was the shock of seeing the story in the *Times*, but basically, he was at a loss to explain his own reaction. As far as Clay was concerned, he cared only about his work and had long ago given up all feeling for his father. "My father made his own bed. He tried to make mine, too. But I refused to lie in it."

Perhaps, Leonard suggested, Clay was lying to himself. His emotional reaction suggested that he really loved his father. Not unnaturally, he had felt he had to assert his own independence, so that he would not fall under his father's sway and be emasculated. He had to kill his father off, but doing that conflicted with his love for his father. Hence the anxiety attacks, and the tearful reaction to his father's fall from power.

Leonard's interpretation seemed to strike a chord with Clay. In thinking back, he was able to see that several of his anxiety attacks had occurred after conversations with or thoughts of Alden. "You know, that's the way a good interpretation is supposed to work," I told Leonard. "It seems familiar to the patient. It's palatable—though maybe not easy to swallow—because it's been there all along."

For a short while after Clay's cathartic session with Leonard, his anxiety attacks diminished. Then they began to return in spades. Both Leonard and I were perplexed. Clay's relationship with Alden Rhodes seemed to have improved. He was able to express his affection for his father, and he had stopped getting angry at every "moral cliché" the old man imparted to him. "I just smile and nod," he told Leonard.

But a new dynamic had entered their relationship. At the same time that Clay became cozier with his father, he shared more and more "insider tips" with Leonard. Most of these tidbits seemed tangential to Clay's actual activities, all except one. Stanton Frank was arranging the merger of two major oil companies, and Clay was the chief architect of the deal. If

Leonard knew which companies were involved, Clay confided, he would be absolutely amazed. "Nobody knows that one of them is in such poor shape," he said.

It was a case of déjà vu. As with the television executive, I pointed out to Leonard that one has to wonder when a patient drops seductive information of this sort. I asked Leonard why he thought Clay had told him about the merger, but he insisted it wasn't important. Clearly, Leonard was afraid to examine the issue with Clay. I remembered how proud he had been that Clay was his first Wall Streeter. Perhaps he couldn't risk upsetting him. Besides, he was clearly enthralled to be hearing about inside stuff, to know things most people have to learn from the newspapers several months after they happen. It might have occurred to him that even his super-successful siblings didn't have entrée to this type of information.

For a competitive, covetous person like Leonard, Wall Street was strewn with land mines. Another patient, the television executive, for example, might tell him something juicy, such as the fact that a new situation comedy could make or break the shaky career of a certain network chief. But what could Leonard do with such information, besides savor it? A Wall Streeter's information, however, could be used for personal gain. I wondered if Leonard had already taken advantage of Clay's tips and bought stock.

Then Leonard told me about a troubling dream that made me realize he hadn't—at least not yet. He told me about the dream because he thought it had something to do with Clay.

In the dream, Leonard was on Long Island, lost "somewhere between Bridgehampton and East Hampton." As he walked along, he looked down and he could see that the earth beneath his feet was caked, with cracks running through it. The terrain was dangerous, although vaguely familiar. Then he came upon a long wall leading up to a house. There was a rooster weather vane on the wall. Leonard wanted the weather vane. He was about to take it when he noticed a police car behind him. A policeman got out of the car and walked toward Leonard, his face shrouded in darkness. Leonard felt both relief and annoyance. He turned away from the policeman and continued to walk down the path.

When Leonard talked about his associations with the dream, we could see that it did indeed have to do with Clay—and me as well. In the dream, Leonard was in the Hamptons, where Clay had a summer home. The caked path on which he walked was a clay road, i.e., Clay Rhodes. Further, Leonard's feeling of being lost confirmed the difficulty he was having in treating Clay. But then the dream shifted to express Leonard's envy. It showed that he wanted not only to treat Clay but to possess what was Clay's. He came to a wall—Wall Street—with an object on it that represented Clay's power and masculinity, the rooster weather vane. In the symbolism of the dream, Leonard was after Clay's financial cock, the wealth he had accumulated on Wall Street.

Leonard was about to give into his desire to take the weather vane when a policeman appeared. That was me. My identity was made clear by the dream's location. The town between Bridgehampton and East Hampton is Wainscott, a homonymous reference to my name. Leonard had mixed feelings toward the policeman. He wanted to be prevented from taking the weather vane, yet he was annoyed. He continued on his original path.

When a therapist dreams of his patient, a countertransference issue is always involved. Although I was not engaged in therapy with Leonard, the dream gave me an opportunity to touch on the subject of his envy, and what it might lead him to do.

Leonard responded with interest to my comments. As usual, he said he was grateful for my help. But this could have been the supervisee game that Leonard played so well. I could only hope that I was getting through to him. His dream was one of envy, crime, and punishment. What disturbed me most was the fact that despite his relief at seeing the policeman, Leonard continued down the same road.

Had I been able to short-circuit this trip? I began to see myself in conflict with Clay for Leonard's spiritual soul. I was to be the loser. I had not reckoned with Clay's pathology-driven persuasiveness. Nor could I have known that the merger of the oil companies was so close at hand.

At Leonard's very next session with Clay, Clay revealed that it would take place within the next few weeks. The stock of the acquired company was certain to rise when the deal went through, he confided to Leonard, and he noted, "insiders" managed to profit by such information "all the time." He insisted on telling Leonard the names of the two companies involved, "so you can understand how big this thing really is." And he started to talk about numbers, numbers which impressed Leonard a great deal.

Clay had upped the ante considerably. Knowing the names of the companies involved in the merger was too much for Leonard to resist. Later that day, he called his broker and purchased the stock of the acquired company. Then he telephoned me and canceled his next session. He had the flu, he said, and would set up another appointment when he felt better.

For the next few weeks, Leonard worried so much that he almost did become sick. He was apprehensive about me, knowing that my reaction was certain to be negative. But, mercenary as he was, his main concern was financial. Supposing he had made a mistake? The stock purchase represented a considerable investment.

It turned out he had little to worry about on that score. As soon as the merger went through, it became clear that Leonard would profit. In fact, the scenario played itself out just as Clay had predicted. Something else had happened, too. Shortly after Leonard told Clay that he had purchased the stock, Clay's anxiety attacks began to diminish.

Clay's improvement gave Leonard the courage to start seeing me again. In reciting the events that had taken place, he looked at me as if he had stumbled on an unusual but effective form of therapy—treatment by greed. I did not hesitate to tell him what I thought. Not only had he done something that was professionally unethical, it was also illegal. I was angry that he had chosen to continue down the pathway in the dream, despite our discussion of the dangers at hand. My major concern, however, was that he had done damage to Clay.

"But Clay's getting better," Leonard protested.

"You've relieved his pain. But only temporarily, I think. The cessation of the attacks shows that Clay was testing you against his father. Alden Rhodes was incorruptible, and he looked down on Clay's business ethics. In the end, though, Alden suffered for his incorruptibility. In transference, you were standing in for Alden. By seducing you—because that's what he did—Clay proved to himself that his father's fall was justified, that the old man's sense of ethics was obsolete."

I told Leonard that colluding with a patient's pathology might lead to short-term gains, but in the long run, it could only make the original problem worse. Clay's anxiety would return, I postulated. And when it did, he would be forced to test the corruptibility of yet another authority figure. Only this time it might not be a therapist, but someone who could prove far more dangerous to his career, such as a boss who was not as admiring as his present superior.

When Leonard first presented Clay to me, he had mentioned that Clay had interviewed other therapists before selecting him, but the others didn't "pan out." Now it seemed that Clay had been subconsciously seeking out a fellow hustler. The fact that the recommendation had come from someone who had met Leonard in a compromising situation, on a vacation with one of his patients, might have given Clay's psyche the clue.

Leonard was chastened by our discussion, and this time I was sure he wasn't simply playing along with me. His face became flushed, and he started to stumble over his words. Part of his discomfiture was satisfying to him, I knew, since I was playing the policeman in his scenario, and Leonard, for all his bravado, felt guilty and had wanted to confess to me.

But now it was time to go beyond guilt, followed by envy, followed by more guilt. Leonard decided to seek out a therapist for himself to get to the bottom of his pattern. At the same time, he knew he would have to confront Clay with the meaning of Clay's behavior, and his own. That would take a large amount of courage. It meant he would have to risk losing Clay. But it also meant that Leonard would be taking a large step forward as a therapist and a human being.

As Leonard feared, Clay terminated treatment shortly after their discussion. I did not hear of Clay again until the end of the eighties, when his name cropped up among those indicted for fraud in the junk-bond scandal. Alden Rhodes had triumphed at last. As for Leonard, after several years of therapy, he went on to achieve the genuine stature that his intelligence, energy, and compassion promised. Perhaps that means he has laid his dream of envy to rest, or at least he has decided to play it out outside of the therapeutic situation, which is where such dreams belong.

CHAPTER 5

The Dream of Rescuing a Damsel in Distress

In the highest tower of an ancient castle, a princess languishes, chained to the wall. A fire-breathing dragon stalks the castle, guarding his unwilling charge. The princess has suffered for a long time, but one day, a knight in armor rides out of the woods. He slays the dragon, scales the tower walls, and rescues the princess. Whether or not he remains with her, he has made it possible for her to live happily ever after.

A wounded knight lies in the woods surrounded by brambles. Although once brave and noble, he is now a shell of his former self. It seems that he will never again be able to slay dragons. But one day, a woman wanders into the woods and fights her way through the brambles. She cares for him until he is once again able to do knightly deeds. Whether or not she remains with him, she has made it possible for him to live happily ever after.

Strip bare the soul of any therapist alive, male or female, and you'll find the desire to rescue someone. It's built into what we do. So it's not surprising that the dream of rescue is one of the most dangerous of countertransference traps. Because it's so natural and compelling, it can blind a therapist to a patient's real problems.

By the time I met Gabriel, he was already deep in this particular trap. In fact, he first called me ten years ago because he had heard I supervised therapists with countertransference problems, and he was "in real trouble." There was one female patient he thought about all the time, he said. "I can't get her out of my mind. She's so vulnerable and sad. She's in a rotten relationship, and she needs help badly. Yet I don't seem to be able to help her enough."

Despite the intensity of Gabriel's feelings, he spoke with a curious detachment. He went on to detail the number of times he had dreamed about his patient and the voluminous notes he was keeping. It was almost as if he was talking about a research project. Then I remembered that Gabriel was a researcher. I had recently seen his name on a paper about a neurobiological approach to depression.

When I mentioned the paper, Gabriel confirmed that research was his basic occupation. He worked at a leading academic hospital and saw only a few patients, for the additional income and the chance to "get out of my ivory tower." The last phrase sounded a bit rueful, as if he had wandered farther from his tower than he intended to. We agreed to get together and discuss his problem.

Gabriel had sounded rather stiff on the telephone, but when I met him, I thought "contained" would be the more appropriate word. He moved carefully and spoke with precision, rather as if he was steering himself through uneasy waters. Yet for all his deliberateness, the way he neatly folded his tweed jacket on the back of a chair, for example, I felt there might be something explosive underneath. Perhaps it was his habit of cracking his knuckles—a sign of suppressed anger— or the way he would sometimes dig his nails into the side of the chair.

Gabriel was in his middle thirties, but his measured manner and a receding hairline made him appear older. So did the slight paunch that was beginning to emerge above his belt, and his nondescript, although neat, clothing. If I had met Gabriel on the street, I thought, I would have taken him for a person who preferred to work with things rather than people.

Yet, Gabriel insisted, he had always been fascinated by people and the motivations for their behavior. That's why he had gone into psychiatry after completing training at a leading medical school. His wife, to whom he had been married for ten years, was a research biologist. They had two children, "both of whom seem to be interested in science, but at their ages, it's difficult to tell about future interests."

Gabriel was brief about his wife and children, and equally brief about his parents. They had lived in Queens for thirty-four years, he said, and ran a neighborhood delicatessen. They were proud of their son's accomplishments. "They insist on showing my articles to everyone who comes in to buy a salami sandwich," he complained, but with more than a hint of pleasure in his voice.

As Gabriel shifted uneasily in his chair, I could see he was anxious to move on to the patient who so concerned him. "When I tell you about Laura—Laura Dawson, her name is— you'll realize the gravity of her situation," he said.

"Tell on," I said lightly, in the hope of relaxing him, but he only became more somber.

"I mean really grave," he reiterated.

Gabriel told me he had been seeing Laura Dawson for three months. From the beginning, he felt he had to rescue her. Life had dealt her so many rough blows, and her present situation was appalling. If she wasn't being physically abused, she was certainly being mentally abused.

The possibility of abuse would have been a concern with any patient, but Laura was so slight and frail, Gabriel said, "as if a strong gust of wind could blow her over." That impression of frailty was a constant of Laura's persona, and it affected Gabriel deeply. It was there no matter how much she changed her appearance, and she made such changes frequently. At each session, she had either a new hair color, a new hairstyle, or a totally different manner of dress. She even experimented with different tones of voice.

At their first session, Laura's hair was black and pulled back in a ponytail, with an unruly set of bangs sweeping down over her eyes. As she brushed the hair back repeatedly, she peered at Gabriel with sad brown eyes. There were circles under those eyes, but they didn't detract from the charm of her delicate, perfectly proportioned features. And strangely, Gabriel didn't find the fact that her nails were bitten almost down to the quick or that she scratched nervously at her wrists unattractive either. These imperfections merely made her more interesting.

Often, new patients will be wary, checking out a therapist as the therapist checks them out. But Laura was almost immediately at ease, telling Gabriel in a low tone that she knew he could help her, he must help her. Every so often she sighed deeply. She had come, she said, because of the persistent feeling "that I'm just a shell with nothing inside." She had had the "shell feeling" since adolescence, but it was growing in strength, and it made her afraid to be alone.

Company didn't always help, she told Gabriel. She also experienced the feeling at home with her live-in boyfriend and on her job. Since graduating from college six years previously, she had been the assistant—"a girl Friday, really"—to a successful commercial artist. She acknowledged the job was a dead end, but she was not ready to leave it. "It's good experience," she maintained. Besides, she had not yet developed any particular career plans.

The job did not pay much, but Laura also had a small inheritance. Her financial situation would have been all right had it not been for Brian, her live-in companion of the last year. He was an unemployed plumber, "sponging off Laura," in Gabriel's opinion, and constantly making her feel insecure by threatening to leave. "No matter how much she gives him, it's never enough," Gabriel commented angrily. "Apparently, he says he'll walk out if he doesn't get what he wants."

Not only did Laura's money feed and clothe Brian, part of it was going to support his nascent coke habit. And he also had a motorcycle to which he was devoted and which seemed to require large amounts of repair. He belonged to a club of cyclists who spent part of each weekend riding around. Even so, Laura idealized Brian. She loved him. He would find worthy employment, she insisted, "when he's ready." In the meantime, Brian was "strong, free, and caring."

Such remarks set Gabriel's teeth on edge. He could readily see that Brian was taking advantage of Laura. "Brian is such a loser," he told me. "Do you know, she often works overtime so he can buy something stupid for that motorcycle? God knows what else he's making her do. Sometimes I feel I'd like to punch him out, pick him up bodily, and toss him out of her life. I've lost my objectivity, to say the least."

Gabriel's anger at Brian and his preoccupation with Laura had led to a repetitive dream. He had never had a repetitive dream before, and it made him anxious, even as he told me about it. "I'm in a darkened house with Laura," he said. "She's sitting in a chair in front of a window, crying. Outside the window, I can see a tree, almost stripped bare of leaves. I'm about to put my arms around Laura to comfort her when I become aware of someone else in the room. It's a tall man in a black leather jacket. I want him out of the house. I walk to the front door and open it, but the man refuses to move. I'm so angry, I want to attack him. That's when I wake up."

Gabriel went on to analyze the dream himself. "The meaning is obvious enough, really. The black leather jacket is probably a motorcycle jacket, standing for Brian. I know that good therapists don't beat up their patients' lovers, so I make myself wake up. But I can't shake off the dream."

Gabriel sank back in the chair, fatigued by his recital. No wonder. His feelings were very turbulent, particularly for a man who valued order. His desire to save Laura from Brian was so strong that he focused on it almost exclusively. Although our session was almost up, he had told me little of Laura's background or the reasons for her "shell feeling." As far as Gabriel was concerned, eliminating Brian would solve whatever problems she might have.

Gabriel had come to me for help, but I wondered if he realized the depth of his countertransference feelings. I doubted that he had ever had any therapy himself. If he had, this issue would almost certainly have been addressed. I suspected, however, that Gabriel wouldn't appreciate being advised to get some therapy. For one thing, his research indicated that he was biologically rather than therapeutically oriented. For another, there was the way he had told me about his dream. Although he called it "obvious," he had avoided opening it up to analysis, thus preventing me from asking about the meaning of the leafless tree, for example. Clearly, his psyche was reserved for himself alone.

Yet even with these thoughts in mind, I was unprepared for the vehemence with which Gabriel greeted my suggestion of therapy. A strong "No" resonated throughout the room, followed by a slow, deliberate shaking of his head. Then silence.

"Surely you realize your countertransference problems are affecting the way you see Laura and Brian?"

More silence.

"Well, if you don't, why did you come to see me?"

"Look, Wayne, I've arrived at the point in my life where I'm comfortable with myself. Although I'm not expressive, I have a good relationship with my wife. We share the same values and interests. We work hard, and we're devoted to our children. I don't want to risk changing any of that."

"You're already at risk, Gabriel. When you called, you said you were 'in trouble.' And from what you've told me today, you were right."

For an instant, Gabriel's usually impassive expression was replaced by terror, as if I had put a gun to his temple. When he spoke, his words were less measured than usual. "All right. I want to keep the lid on, always have wanted to since I was a small child. I don't know what it is I'm sitting on—or we wouldn't be having this conversation, would we—but I do know I have to sit tight."

We had come to an impasse. I was about to suggest that Gabriel consult someone else about his problem with Laura, when he had an idea. Since I would be supervising him, why couldn't I provide a kind of quasi therapy at the same time? After all, in discussing his treatment of his patients, we could well uncover personal issues of his own.

I knew immediately that the suggestion was a poor one. It's not possible to be someone's therapist and supervisor at the same time. And even if it were, I suspected that what Gabriel really wanted was tranquilizing—verbal Valium—rather than therapy. Yet I found myself agreeing to do it. It was unlikely that Gabriel would seek out another therapist, I rationalized, and Laura would inevitably suffer from his flawed skills. Besides, he was clearly so unhappy.

Thus I, too, was slipping into the rescue fantasy, only I would be rescuing the therapist, rather than the patient. But as a medical person, it certainly was not the first time I had cast myself in that role. It's common to the breed.

So while I agreed to Gabriel's plan, I recognized the dangers and laid down some ground rules. We would undertake the project on a trial basis for two months. And by the next session, I wanted to know a whole lot more about Laura. Why was she so thin and "frail"? Could she be suffering from anorexia? Was she, too, a drug user, as the companions of users frequently are? Gabriel looked at me solemnly, pulled out a black notebook, and jotted something down, as if undertaking a research project.

My "assignment" was intended to get Gabriel thinking about Laura, rather than Brian, but his first words at our next session were, "Brian is a terrible person, Wayne. I wish I could make you see that."

I said nothing.

After giving me a look that suggested "so this is what it feels like to be in therapy," Gabriel at last told me Laura's history. And as I listened, I could see why the events in her life might indeed evoke a need to rescue.

Laura Dawson grew up in Ohio, the only child of a rural physician and his former receptionist. She remembered being very close to both parents. In spite of his duties at the hospital, her father spent a great deal of time with her, and until the age of seven, her childhood was a normal one.

On Laura's seventh birthday, her father was killed in a car crash. He was, in fact, hurrying home to her party when the accident occurred. Laura had a vivid memory of the police car arriving at the house, her mother's ashen face as the policemen spoke with her, and all of the children being sent home before the cake was served or the presents opened.

Laura was overwhelmed. She escaped by going into a corner and looking at her favorite picture book. One of the policemen asked her whether she was all right, and she said quite decidedly that she was. But of course, neither Laura nor her mother was all right. The mother sank into a depression that lasted over a year. And Laura became increasingly clingy. She didn't like to let her mother out of her sight.

Two years after her father's death, Laura's mother was also killed. Leaving the local bank, she was hit by scaffolding falling from an adjacent building. Everyone called it a "freak accident," but somehow Laura wasn't surprised. She had begun to expect to lose those close to her.

Laura went to live with her widowed maternal grandmother on a farm nearby. Her grandmother, a kindly woman, was nonetheless severely taxed by the demands of taking care of a child. As Laura grew into adolescence, she learned to keep her needs pretty much to herself, lest her grandmother find her too annoying and be unable to keep her.

Then a few months before Laura left for college, her grandmother suffered a heart attack. Laura was alone in the house with her and by the time the local ambulance corps arrived in response to the girl's call, her grandmother was dead.

During her school vacations, Laura stayed with an assortment of cousins. One of them helped her manage her meager inheritance. Although everyone was kind, Laura realized she was on her own. She experienced widespread mood swings, either feeling "on top of the world" or intensely depressed or angry.

In college and afterwards, Laura experimented sexually with both men and women, often without intending to do so. She would cuddle up with a woman friend, "just to be close friendly," and wind up being masturbated to orgasm. She would chat with a boy at the library and then "find herself" spending the night in his room. These experiences, she remembered, helped to alleviate her growing sense of "being just a shell."

There were several longer-term relationships with men. In each case, the young man seemed perfect, but at a certain point, something went wrong. One lover was an aspiring politician, who decided that Laura lacked the drive to be his life's partner. Another was an entrepreneurial type, who became annoyed by Laura's lack of interest in his business.

As Laura told it, she was constantly being abandoned by men, until Brian came on the scene. They had been together for more than a year, her longest relationship to date. Since meeting Brian, she had actually put on some weight—she had always been naturally thin—and thus far, she felt no interest in getting involved in cocaine use. But supporting both Brian and his habit were "no trouble," she insisted, even if she had to stray outside the law occasionally to do it. She sometimes indulged in petty shoplifting so she had extra cash for Brian, she told Gabriel. "Brian's worth it. I know he'll always be there for me."

When Gabriel finished his story, he turned the full force of his blue eyes on me as if to indicate that he had covered everything on my agenda, and it all came back down to Brian.

"What do you make of Laura's situation? I mean before she met Brian," I said.

"Well, her background makes it easy to understand why she has a fear of being abandoned. Fear is a weak word, really. She has a positive terror of it. She sometimes telephones me several times before an appointment, just to make certain I'll actually be there. That's why she allows herself to be victimized by Brian, I think, because he represents a safe haven."

I concurred that Laura was seeking safety. She must have a fantasy of herself as Typhoid Mary, in that her love kills those who are exposed to her. I also suggested to Gabriel that Laura fit the clinical description of a patient with a borderline personality disorder. Occasionally, people with this disorder have, like Laura, experienced a great many losses. Their sense of identity is shaky, and they are unable to establish a firm choice of career. Like Laura, they claim they are satisfied with "assistant-type" jobs. Some borderline personalities constantly change their image in order to please the people they are with—hence Laura's changes in appearance and tone of voice. And as a final characteristic, to stave off their dread of being alone, borderline personalities may undertake a series of intense but unstable personal relationships.

Gabriel considered these points solemnly, as was his habit. But borderline or not, in his view, the problem still centered around Brian. By exploiting Laura, he was exacerbating her difficulties. In Gabriel's view, the difficulties could be alleviated by following one prescription: "Laura needs to get rid of Brian."

I wondered if Gabriel's inability to focus on Laura rather than Brian meant he was suppressing something in his own history that might resonate with hers. Problems with a patient often point to parallels between the patient's past and the therapist's. Since abandonment was a big issue in Laura's life, I asked Gabriel whether, as a child, he had ever feared he might be abandoned by his parents.

"Never," said Gabriel, with some satisfaction. "My parents are both as solid as rocks. That delicatessen I told you about —they've been running it since 1946, the year I was born. In fact, when I was younger, we lived above the store. Oh, it was a struggle for them. Especially for Mom, being on her feet all day. She's slightly crippled. But no matter how hard they worked, they always made me feel secure. They're absolutely devoted to each other. No marital problems that I've ever known of."

With that, Gabriel stared off into space. He could not have made himself clearer if he had said, "And they never needed any rescuing either, thank you." He really was keeping that lid on, I reflected. I saw now that I was correct in thinking our quasi-therapeutic relationship might be untenable. A lawyer who defends himself, they say, has a fool for a client. So where does that leave a therapist who agrees to sort of treat another therapist who really doesn't want to be treated? Not getting anywhere, I concluded over the next few weeks, as Gabriel continued to harp on Brian and resist most of my attempts to discuss his own past. If anything, he was more open about his relationship with his wife—which did seem to be a good one —then he was about his parents.

The lid, I conjectured, probably had something to do with them. But what? If his father had been abusive toward his mother, thus giving Gabriel a desire to "rescue" her, it was not something that could easily be denied. After all, this couple was together all the time; an abusive relationship would hardly go unnoticed by their son. I remembered my own father's furious tirades and how they had filled me with terror from early childhood on. There was no way I could have overlooked them. Perhaps Gabriel's inability to articulate the problem with Laura meant it had to do with a feeling he connected to his parents. But what was there about this ordinary, hard-working couple that could have created such complete denial?

I had a notion I would never know by the time the two-month trial period was up. But just as our relationship was coming near its end, Laura's relationship with Brian appeared to take the turn that Gabriel feared most.

"He's beating her," he announced one day.

Laura had come to a session in a disheveled state. When she greeted Gabriel, she spoke in a throaty whisper, the tone Gabriel had once characterized as her "Jackie Kennedy voice." She stood facing him for a few moments, saying nothing. Then she hiked up her blouse so that he could see a series of bruises on her abdomen, as if a deliberate pattern had been created with a blunt instrument. The marks were all the more appalling because the body on which they had been inflicted was so slight.

Laura quickly rearranged her clothing, sat down, and started to cry softly. "I wanted to comfort her and kill Brian at the same time," Gabriel said, cracking his knuckles.

"Anything else?"

The searchlights of his blue eyes ran over me. "I was sexually aroused, too. I won't deny it. In fact, it was one of the strongest sexual feelings I've ever had in my life. I wanted to take her then and there. I wanted to rub my hands along her stomach and obliterate every damn mark that bastard had made."

Therapeutically, I was pleased by Gabriel's honesty. It hadn't been difficult to guess his reaction to the scene with Laura. The dream of rescuing a damsel in distress is in itself sexually compelling. A "distressed" woman's vulnerability makes her attractive and at the same time nonthreatening. A man need not fear she might reject him. He can allow his feelings for her to surface.

As an ethical therapist, Gabriel could not act on his impulses toward Laura. But he did everything he could to comfort her with words. Yet for all her distress, Laura declined to admit that Brian had attacked her. She was very angry at Brian "for being such a creep." But when Gabriel suggested that she make immediate plans to leave him, she refused and became furious at Gabriel.

"I thought you understood me," she screamed in a high-pitched voice. "Leave Brian? Damn! You shrinks don't know what the hell you're talking about."

For the rest of the session, Laura put down almost everything Gabriel said, and when she left, she slammed the door behind her. Gabriel worried that she might never return. "Laura needs security so badly, she'll even put up with being hurt by that Nazi to get it. If she doesn't come back, I might never be able to convince her to leave Brian."

Gabriel's choice of the word "Nazi" was evocative. I was going to discuss it with him, when I realized how preoccupied he was by Laura's last visit. His dream of rescuing her had hit an impasse at the very time his notion that she was in danger had been confirmed.

If Laura was indeed a battered woman, Gabriel was correct in advising her to leave the relationship at once, and in discussing practical details as to where she might go and when. Yet there was another way to consider their last session, and that was in the light of the borderline personality disorder diagnosis. People with this disorder tend to idealize those they are close to, then become intensely angry at them for seemingly minor reasons. We didn't know why Laura's earlier relationships had ended. She said her lovers had abandoned her, but she may have dismissed them in anger.

Now Laura seemed to be turning on both Brian and Gabriel. Gabriel had done nothing to incite her fury. It seemed that Brian had. But then again, perhaps he had not. Borderline personalities are also self-destructive and given to self-mutilation. By mutilating themselves they delineate boundaries. Pain lets them know where they leave off and the world begins.

I reminded Gabriel that when we first met he had described Laura's bitten nails and her habit of mutilating herself by scratching furiously at her wrists. Perhaps, in a fit of rage at Brian over some incident or other, she herself had inflicted the bruises on her abdomen. It was just a hypothesis, of course, but either way, Laura was in danger. If I was correct, another self-destructive act could occur. If Gabriel was correct, she could be severely injured, or worse, by a violent lover. We agreed that Gabriel would telephone Laura and urge her to keep her next appointment.

Although Gabriel was behaving in a thoroughly rational manner, I knew he was seething inside. I thought about his "lid." Would it pop if something happened to Laura? I suspected that deep down Gabriel had feelings as violent as those he attributed to Brian. He could, in fact, be projecting that violence onto Brian, hence his choice of the appellation "Nazi." Or, perhaps his intuition had been correct to begin with, and Brian was a dangerous person. After all, the physical evidence seemed to point in that direction. Yet somehow my intuition said no.

I responded to this uneasy situation by sleeping poorly and worrying a great deal for the next several days. It turned out that I had reason to worry. Laura didn't keep her next appointment with Gabriel. In response to his call, she had begrudgingly agreed to see him. He even had his secretary send her an additional appointment card for emphasis. Still, she failed to show up. But later that evening, Gabriel was contacted by the emergency room of an uptown hospital. Laura had been injured in a motorcycle accident and had been brought there, unconscious and alone. His appointment card was one of the few items found on her person.

By the time Gabriel arrived at the hospital, Laura had regained consciousness, but the emergency room doctor took him aside before he could see her. Although Laura's injuries in the crash seemed to be limited to a concussion, he had noticed the contusions on her abdomen and the scratches on her wrists, and was concerned that these bruises could be the result of abuse.

Laura had vehemently denied that possibility, but battered women frequently deny that they have been abused. Gabriel agreed that abuse was a distinct possibility. He was pleased, he later told me, as he watched the physician write on the chart "Some injuries suggestive of battering." Now, he thought, Brian's activities were part of the medical record, and other professionals might advise Laura to leave him.

Just as the doctor finished writing, a slightly built man with sandy-colored hair and a worried expression appeared in the doorway. He was dressed in jeans, a worn plaid jacket, and workboots. His wind-tossed hair and granny eyeglasses, slightly askew, contributed to the unsettled look on his face.

It was Brian. He had been going from hospital to hospital in search of Laura who, he said, had been missing for more than a day, along with his motorcycle. It wasn't the first time she had raced off recklessly on the cycle, nor was this her first crack-up. Until now, however, she had gotten off with relatively minor injuries.

Gabriel was speechless. For months, he had pictured Brian as a Hell's Angel. Not only didn't he fit the stereotype, his manner was gentle and soft-spoken. In spite of his concern about Laura's condition, he seemed genuinely pleased to meet Gabriel and expressed gratitude for "all you've been trying to do." However, Brian's current amiability didn't mean he couldn't have been violent at some point. In fact, after an abuser has released tension by attacking a woman, he typically enters a phase of being "nice." The "honeymoon period" is the term used by therapists who work with battered women.

The emergency room physician wondered aloud if Brian might know something about the marks on Laura's abdomen. The man stared at the floor, as if ashamed. Then he murmured something that was too low to hear. Asked to repeat himself, he raised his head and looked directly at Gabriel. "I made a terrible mistake," he said. "I wasn't there to prevent it."

He and Laura had been arguing about her therapy, Brian told them. "You should tell the doctor about the things you do to yourself," he insisted. "Otherwise he can't help you."

When Laura demurred, Brian stalked out to have a few drinks with his friends. He returned a few hours later to find Laura huddled on the bed, a small lead pipe lying nearby. After he left, she said, she had pulled the pipe out of his plumber's kit and struck herself repeatedly on the abdomen. It was his fault, she said, for "walking out" on her.

Laura's moods had always been volatile, Brian explained, but lately she had become more reckless than ever. She had, for example, taken to shoplifting small items from stores "just for the hell of it," even though he warned her she was certain to get caught.

At the beginning of their relationship, Laura had thought him godlike, and that was very rewarding for Brian. He said he had "a small problem with cocaine," hadn't been able to hold a job, and tended to see himself as a loser. Laura, however, saw him as sensitive and simply too good for this world. But within the last few weeks, her view of him had changed dramatically. He seemed to have failed her in some way. She accused him of planning to leave. He had despaired of ever making her happy again. "She hasn't been easy to deal with, I can tell you that, but I would never, never leave her," Brian concluded emphatically.

When Gabriel got in to see Laura, she was still groggy from the injury. The sight of her lying there on a hospital bed, helpless, a white sheet carelessly pulled up around her, aroused him sexually, he admitted. Once more, he felt a strong need to take care of her, to make up for whatever deed had brought her here, even if it was self-inflicted.

Laura, however, was having none of him. At first, she turned her face to the wall, as if that might make him go away. When it didn't, she rolled over on her back and addressed the ceiling. "I didn't ask you to come. I'm getting another therapist, one who won't run out on me."

"I haven't run out on you, Laura."

"Fuck you."

She refused to say anything further to Gabriel. Instead, she rang for the nurse and asked if Brian was there. She seemed delighted that he had managed to find her, and demanded to see him immediately.

Later, the emergency room physician told Gabriel that Laura had continue to deny being battered. She also denied Brian's story that her wounds were self-inflicted. So the physician amended his notes to read "injuries suggestive of battering or self-mutilation."

That was where Gabriel had to leave it, at the word "suggestive." He realized that he might never know the truth of what had happened between Laura and Brian. But he did see the truth of his own fantasy. Laura was a "damsel in distress" all right. But she did not need a therapist who wanted to rescue her. She needed a therapist who could help her work through her past.

Gabriel admitted all of this to me as he described his shock at meeting the real Brian. "There was no doubt in my mind. I was absolutely certain of what he would look like, what he would sound like. But he wasn't a Nazi after all."

"No black leather jacket?"

"There may be one in his closet someplace, but somehow I tend to doubt it." It was the first time I had seen Gabriel grin. In spite of his failure in treating Laura, he looked as if a weight had fallen from his shoulders. And all because Brian might not be the fascist he had imagined him to be.

"This isn't the first time you've brought up the word 'Nazi,' " I said.

"Okay, I'm Jewish, so I certainly have strong feelings about Nazis."

"Anything else?"

I could see Gabriel pulling into himself, like a snail moving into its shell. I had a feeling I was getting close to the "lid." "I really think we should talk about why the idea of rescue is so important to you," I said.

"My parents are concentration camp survivors. They were both in Auschwitz," Gabriel said. "I've never thought about rescue in connection with them, though. They are both such strong people. But I always felt very different from other children, because of what had happened to them. I thought I had to make it up to them by being very good and successful. Things in our house weren't like they were in other houses. It was a feeling I could never pin down."

His parents rarely talked about the war, he told me. It was as if they had put a lid on the subject, a lid Gabriel was forced to accept. He understood that questions weren't welcome. Yet he knew there was something terrible in their past. "There was a skinny little girl next door who always used to ask why my mother had that number on her arm," he recalled, cracking his knuckles. "When I asked my mother, she said it was something that happened 'in the camp.' And that was that. I had the feeling that if I pushed her further, a bomb would go off."

At the time Gabriel and I saw each other, research was just starting to come out about the psychological burden carried by the children of concentration camp survivors. Many, like Gabriel, reported feelings of being different, of wanting to make it up to their parents for their past experiences, and of keeping something bottled up inside. Some quite explicitly reported a wish to "rescue" their parents, to prevent what had happened to them from happening.

When I raised these points with Gabriel, an expression of relief came over his face. For the first time, it seemed, he realized he was not alone with his feelings or his "lid." Gabriel remembered that about a year before he began treating Laura, he had taken his mother to see a colleague, a surgeon who was going to operate on her for a wrist ailment. When the doctor casually asked why his mother's right leg was shorter than the left, Gabriel learned for the first time that it had been broken by a guard "in the camp" and, not being set, had failed to heal properly.

Gabriel had been filled with rage, he told me. If he could have gotten his hands on that guard, he would have torn the man into small pieces. At the same time, he felt himself trying to push the lid back on, because part of his anger, he realized as we talked, concerned his father. His father, too, had been in the camp, yet he had been unable to protect his mother. Rationally, Gabriel knew that his father was helpless, a victim himself, and that he was probably nowhere near Gabriel's mother at the time of the incident. Nevertheless, he had somehow failed to save her.

As he recalled his feelings about his parents, Gabriel began to see that in undertaking to rescue Laura, he might have projected onto her a subconscious wish to rescue his mother. The frail, weeping woman he wanted to comfort in the dream he recounted at our first session probably represented both his mother and Laura. And the lifeless tree outside the window could have been his family tree, which had almost totally been stripped bare of leaves. Gabriel was unaware of having any relatives other than his parents, although this, too, had never been discussed. He knew he was just about the only remaining leaf on the tree. That was a big responsibility. It meant that he had to rescue the future as well as the past.

Although our conversation that day had been quite a beginning, Gabriel realized we had just begun to pry at the top of his lid. More suppressed material came to mind. He had been given the name Gabriel—the name of a rescuing archangel, by the way—after an unidentified dead relative. Now, he realized, he had always wondered if his parents had any other children, children who might have been killed "in the camp." Perhaps one of them was his namesake.

Because so much was coming to the surface, and there were so many unanswered questions, Gabriel gave up any further attempt to "rescue" Laura. He also knew he had to confront his parents at some point. To help him in doing that and in understanding his feelings, he knew he would need therapy.

Gabriel not only went into treatment, he became active in a support group for the children of concentration camp survivors. The group has become a central force in his life, enabling him to connect with other people who have had experiences similar to his. An avid researcher, it is not surprising that he is now an expert on the subject and frequently addresses groups of therapists. He continues to treat a small number of patients but, as far as I know, he has put away his knightly steed. His desire to rescue damsels in distress is under control.

CHAPTER 6

The Dream of Letting Go

In this age of sexual freedom, it may be hard to imagine that any of us could grow up to feel barred from sexual experience. Yet there are unfortunate men and women who, however powerfully drawn to that world of human pleasure, only dream of entering it, of letting themselves go sexually as others do. A therapist caught in this dream is all too likely to exploit a patient to further it, and may even, as in the case of Stan, briefly manage to beguile a supervisor with it as well.

Beguiling was, however, not a word I would have used to describe the bulky man who shambled into my office one afternoon in the early 1970s. I looked from his frayed collar to the button dangling from his jacket sleeve to the drooping socks and thick rubber-soled shoes with their knotted shoelaces, and was immediately put off. He was in his early thirties, just a few years younger than I, but he struck me as alien, a relic of some other time. His basic outfit—tweed jacket, Shetland sweater, corduroy pants, argyle socks—was, in its disrepair, a parody of the clothes college professors wore back in the 1950s. Yet the face under the unfashionable crewcut was preternaturally youthful, untouched by the struggles and passions most of us have lived through by his age.

On the surface, Stan didn't seem to offer much as a supervisee. Almost at once I despaired of finding a hook to sink into him to engage my interest, as I usually try to do when I don't feel immediately able to relate to a supervisee or a patient. Stan discouraged me even further by his opening chitchat on the five-day weather forecast. He spoke in an exaggerated, almost mock New York accent, not the smooth one of the Upper East Side but the rasping one Jimmy Cagney made famous. As a native New Yorker, I relished the city's medley of accents, but Stan's irritated me as much as did his general appearance.

It was through this case that I would learn for all time the error of such facile judgmentalism, for it was as inappropriate a response to my supervisee as it would be to any patient. But at that time I had not been a supervisor all that long, and there was still one important area in my own life that I had not really confronted. Thus with Stan, rather than being alerted by my bias against him, I hunkered down to endure him. I very much regretted having let an older colleague persuade me to take him on, saying that my approach might be just the thing for him. I had acquiesced out of respect for this psychiatrist, although he relied heavily on medication as opposed to my psychodynamic approach and was very different in style. At the hospital where he and I both taught, he had something of a reputation as a tartar. He was also on the staff of the hospital where Stan had trained as a psychiatrist, a good enough institution in its way but, like my colleague, oriented toward psychopharmacology.

To begin with, Stan presented me with no particular problem in his practice but simply gave me a rundown on his patients, a group I soon came to feel he had selected for their blandness and banality, qualities Stan himself exhibited in the extreme. He simply droned on and on, expressing little real interest in his patients or in his solutions to their problems. For all the animation he showed, they might have been someone else's patients and he merely the neutral recorder of their cases.

One afternoon after a few such sessions with Stan, I found myself stifling a yawn and wondered whether I was going to be able to keep awake. I had had a big lunch and the lure of a postprandial nap fought with my conscience as an attentive supervisor. I hoped Stan had not noticed the few times I had actually caught myself nodding in recent sessions, and I wished I could devise some way to liven him up.

At that moment, as if he had sensed my wish, he wound up the case that had inspired my yawn and introduced a new patient, a young woman. "Samantha's sort of a leftover flower child," he said in his grating voice.

Then, as my eyes must have focused rather abruptly, Samantha being clearly out of a more mixed bag than Stan's previous humdrum patients, he went on with a nod and a sudden smile. "And she's got a face like a pre-Raphaelite Madonna on a real Marilyn Monroe body!"

With those few words, Stan's whole aspect altered. His eyes gleamed. His body's usual bloblike contours gained definition. His clothes suddenly didn't look so tacky and out of another age. Even his voice had a lilt. His smile was pure delight, and tickled me to no end with its hint of gleeful guilt, like the proverbial small boy caught with his hand in the cookie jar. Maybe Stan was not such a dull dog after all, I thought. There may be a way to connect with him yet.

I had no trouble keeping from yawning for the rest of the session, as Stan launched into Samantha's story, his face lighting up whenever he mentioned her name. Born on Beacon Hill to a clan of Boston Brahmins, she was the only daughter and fourth child of a family where sons were prized. Her three brothers had all gone the prescribed route through Exeter and on to Harvard, and she, too, back in the middle 1960s, appeared to be following convention when she enrolled at Wellesley. Then almost overnight all that changed, and along with many others of her generation, she dropped out of college and out of the world her family knew. After seven years of wandering, in Europe at first and then the Far East, she was now living in Greenwich Village, a refugee from a crash pad in the Haight-Ashbury section of San Francisco.

As Stan related these details, I noted a certain incredulity in his voice, a bemusement that anyone could get away with such an irregular and outlandish life. For Samantha had been flitting not merely from country to country but from lover to lover as well. By this time her family had pretty well given up on helping her, and only a modest trust fund stood between her and Skid Row.

Stan told me she had been to several therapists over the years but stayed with none more than a few months. With her most recent therapist, a pastoral counselor whom she had sought out after hearing him speak at an anti–Vietnam War rally in San Francisco, she had had an affair, but eventually he had abandoned her. Thus, she clearly had difficulty forming trusting relationships and probably tended to turn most relationships with men into sexual ones. Had Stan possessed an overt sexual presence, I doubt her treatment with him would have gotten off the ground. As it was, however, she felt free to talk to him about her search for the right man, which she saw as the main problem of her life. Like most of us, she was seeking someone who was both sexually desirable and had a mind and interests she could admire. But in her case the men she had met over the years who seemed initially to fill the bill either turned out to be crucially lacking in one or the other respect, or didn't want a long-term relationship.

As Stan recounted his sessions with Samantha, I was struck by her consistent lack of introspection. What's past is past, she stated in both words and manner, according to Stan, her voice empty of emotion in speaking of the men she had known, including her recent therapist-lover, in sharp contrast to her excitement when speaking of a current or potential lover. As she saw her life, things simply happened to her and that was that. Reasons were irrelevant.

Listening to Stan describe this aspect of her personality, I wondered whether there was any chance of Samantha's benefiting from therapy, whether the therapy could progress at all, if she had so little ability or desire to acknowledge her own contribution to her life situation. When I mentioned this doubt to Stan, he brushed it aside and spoke enthusiastically about her brightness and potential. It was clear that in his eyes, his liking for her and desire to help her were sufficient guarantees of success and outweighed the reality of her case. I was astonished by his attitude, more appropriate to an adolescent than an experienced therapist, but I recognized that to such cockeyed optimism my warnings would seem like the ravings of Cassandra. I decided that at this early stage it was probably wise to wait and see how Stan would actually deal with his fascinating patient.

Then began a strange period in the supervision. As the weeks passed, our sessions took on a predictable pattern. Stan would come in, ease his bulk into the chair across from me, lean forward briefly to scan his notes, and then sit back and relate in detail the latest in the series of Samantha's amatory adventures. He told me she had persuaded the superintendent of her building to send someone to fix her toilet or kitchen sink, and I couldn't help but be amused to hear that when a handyman finally came she promptly jumped into bed with him. Or be diverted when the next week the handyman's sexual derring-do was replaced by the marijuana dealer's or, the following week, by a lusty Ayn Randian advocate she had met at a Village bookstore. Week after week, Stan presented another plum from Samantha's apparently endless cornucopia of earthy delights, a saga to rival any dreamed up by Anaïs Nin or Henry Miller.

Of course, in ordinary supervision a certain amount of detail about a patient's sexual life usually emerges, along with information about his or her working life, family, and so on. In Samantha's case, however, the sexual side of her life and her therapy sessions were threatening to overwhelm the supervision. Furthermore, it was a situation I was doing nothing to avert. Then one day after an especially tedious opening, Stan became bogged down in telling me about some verbal altercation between Samantha and the owner of a laundromat. Suddenly I caught myself actually wishing he would get to the point, that is to Samantha's latest sexual turn, as it was a good bet all this was leading up to her going to bed with the fellow. I was wondering, in fact, when Stan would *reward* me, when he would gratify *me!*

This realization was deeply disturbing. In its wake, I had to acknowledge to myself several uncomfortable truths. First, that I had for some time been unconsciously accepting Stan's tales of Samantha's sexual shenanigans as a reasonable recompense for spending my time in these excruciatingly boring sessions with a therapist who seemed pretty much of a dud. Second, that under the guise of a helping psychotherapy, a covert crime was taking place, one to which I was an accessory. And finally, that Stan and I were co-conspirators in supervisory sessions that were diverting but were no more enlightening than the movie thrillers whose latest installment I used to look forward to in the Saturday afternoons of my boyhood. In other words, the supervision had gotten way out of hand.

There was no point in interrupting Stan's narration and bringing up the matter then and there. Before I could do that, I had to think seriously about what was really going on between the two of us. After our session ended that day, I wondered what was behind my passive response to him. Was I unconsciously displacing onto him some need, some unfinished business of my own? I briefly tried to comfort myself with the thought that however gratifying and wonderful my own marriage was, it was hard not to be fascinated by the ways other people can disport themselves sexually in the world of apparently endless choice outside marriage. But, of course, that was no excuse at all, and was, in any case, a minor factor in my straying from the path of supervisory neutrality.

Then I tried to think about Stan himself and realized that I thought about him as little as possible. Nothing had so far changed my original perception of him as being a sort of neuter being, a sexual nonentity, an antiquated alien. That perception had blocked out any more realistic perception of him, had even blocked me from seeking one. Why had I let that happen so easily? Why had I wanted to see him only as the neuter blob he presented to the world?

I visualized Stan as he had been that day: not one but two missing buttons on his shirt, the beginnings of another hole in his sweater, his air of youth belied by his premature middle-aged spread. In contrast to Samantha, who had given herself to the 1960s with all its freedoms and attendant vicissitudes, that decade seemed to have washed over him with some caustic substance that eroded his clothes and left him all but frozen in his tracks. I heard again in my mind the unnatural accent in his voice. And suddenly the thought hit home, evoking painful echoes of my one and only sibling, my older brother.

Growing up, I had idolized George. When I was a kid, not yet a teenager, he had told me my first dirty joke and a bit later answered my questions about sex. More important, he bore the brunt of my father's angry tirades, thus making my own childhood easier but at a terrible cost to himself. When George joined the Navy during the Second World War, I missed him keenly. And when he came home after the war, I was overjoyed, especially when I was the only member of the family there the day he walked in the front door. He gave me a big bear hug and then sat down with me and opened the bottle of whiskey he had brought with him. That afternoon the two of us got drunk together, as he regaled me with one war story after another. Afterward, he held my head when I puked up my guts in the bathroom. I dearly loved him then and I wanted to be a man like him.

As I went on to college and medical school, however, my idol proved all too soon to have feet of clay, and his reality came less and less to match the image in my heart. Instead of being able to understand his inner turmoil and unending struggles to reconcile the immense potential within him with the anger that drove his outward behavior, I was furious at him for disappointing me, for not measuring up to what I wanted him to be. It was as if I felt his sole task was to be there for me to look up to. I resented his leaving me to do and discover so many things on my own. Dammit, George, I would think, the few times I now saw him, why did you have to change? Why couldn't you have stayed as you were?

At this period of my life, I had been out of touch with George for some time. I certainly didn't like to be reminded of him, and hence avoided seeing Stan's resemblance to him. He, like Stan, seemed stuck in a time warp, somewhere back in the late 1940s, when he had last felt alive and vital. He, too, had an irritating accent that seemed to call attention to his dismal state.

This insight into the basis of my bias against Stan enabled me to recognize how little I had been with him during the supervisory sessions. In order to spare myself the pain of once again recognizing my disappointment in my older brother, I had tuned out and distanced myself from the emotions Stan was arousing in me. And thus I had tuned out an important feeling I should have long since been aware of in the supervision—that is, the pleasure I experienced from listening to him relate the weekly episodes of "Samantha's Sexual Saga." This reprise of the dirty jokes and sexual enlightenment my brother had offered me as a youngster allowed me to overlook my own failure as a supervisor in respect to a supervisee who, I now suspected, was very needy—just as that macho bonding ritual had enabled me to overlook George's inadequacies and to idealize him long beyond the time such idealization was necessary or useful.

It took some weeks of internal struggle for me to work out the implications of the connection between Stan and my brother. Now it was high time I took hold of the supervisory sessions and got them back on the track. I opened the next one myself, before Stan had a chance to take out his notes. I thought it best to begin by bluntly pointing out to him the fact that, since he had started in on Samantha's case, almost all of our sessions had culminated in one or another of her sexual exploits. "Now, though I recognize that sex is an important part of her life, it's come to dominate the supervision and, I suspect, your therapy sessions with her as well. Have you any thoughts about why that's happened?"

As I spoke, Stan's usual air of being almost bursting with what he had to tell me slowly faded. I had the distinct impression of having pricked the balloon of his fantasy, even to the slow expiration of breath he let out from between pursed lips. After a long pause, he finally asked, "Isn't a patient's sexual life supposed to be the focus of their psychotherapy?"

"*A* focus, but not necessarily the only one."

Again Stan hesitated, almost visibly sorting through his thoughts. I waited for him to speak.

"I thought I was doing the right thing with her and with you," he finally muttered defensively. "Now you tell me I'm not. What—"

"That's not exactly what I said," I interrupted. "I'm asking whether your preoccupation with Samantha's sexuality in your sessions both with her and with me hasn't served to screen out other important factors in her life history that she may find it painful to address. Factors that we should have been recognizing and discussing here." I paused as he looked at me blankly.

"What do you think?" I asked again.

"Are you saying," he murmured so softly I could hardly hear him, "I've got some countertransference block that's interfering with the treatment?"

I nodded. "Actually, that wasn't my first thought, though I have the feeling it's true. And isn't it possible, Stan, that that's what you're here to explore?" He looked away and I determinedly returned to my original tack. "I believe that Samantha has been offering up her sexuality to you in order to keep you away from other areas of her personality. That is," I added to goad him, "if you think there's anything to her beyond her sexuality. I'm not so sure."

Stan straightened in his chair. "Come off it, Wayne! She's got more on the ball than you give her credit for."

"That may be, Stan," I said slowly and deliberately, "but you haven't really told me about it, have you?"

As we stared at one another, Stan's face worked convulsively for a moment, as if he was about to cry. For the first time, I felt a pang of compassion for him. Softening my tone, I explained that however strong I may have come on, I had no intention of trying to attack him. I pointed out that somehow we had let the therapy and the supervision become one-sided, and now we had to try to figure out why that had happened.

For the rest of our time that day and the next several sessions, we examined Stan's detailed process notes of Samantha's therapy hours. But his notes added nothing to what he had already reported in previous supervisory hours. They confirmed my supposition that he was not delving beyond sex in his treatment of Samantha, and provided little insight into either his countertransference or the young woman herself.

Again, I knew I was missing something, but wasn't sure just how to get at it. I felt it might be useful to go back to my original insight into the connection between Stan and my brother. I thought of how, as I got older, George gradually realized not only that he had disappointed me but also that he sorely needed my love and admiration. Thus he pandered to my sexual curiosity, always having some raunchy story or joke to tell me the few times we got together, in an effort to repeat the macho male bonding ritual that had worked in the past when I was a kid.

I wondered how that related to Stan. I suspected that he had come to me originally not merely for supervisory help but to loosen himself up in some way. Indeed, he must have been as bored as I was with those bland patients he first presented. Then, sensing my negative response, he had switched to Samantha to recapture my interest and had succeeded because his attempt echoed in my mind my brother's attempts to regain my admiration.

So far so good. Only the picture was still incomplete. How had Stan kept my interest so long?

I decided at our next session to let him revert to his old mode of presentation and describe Samantha's approach to her latest lover. As I listened, I began to recognize something about his style I hadn't been aware of. His tendency to skip around in his reports, leaving out a detail here, backtracking to another there, was an all too effective way of ensnaring my attention, of teasing me, of getting me to feel at the moment his own arousal, his own urge to let go in respect to Samantha during the therapy hour with her. I now realized that his descriptions of her sexual activities had a sort of story-telling quality. They were a little like a pornographic novel in seeming to build up to one seduction scene after another. But not hard-core porn by any means. No, his circuitous buildup became a sort of foreplay that seemed as if it would never get to the climax, and as the listener, I was all but begging for its orgasmic conclusion.

Once I had worked all this out, the session was nearly over. But I took the last few minutes to share my thoughts with him. "To put it another way," I wound up, "it's as though you're unconsciously trying to arouse me as you let Samantha arouse you in your therapy sessions with her."

As I spoke Stan's expression had grown ever more still. When I finished, he got up. "I can't believe any supervisor would ever say such a bizarre thing! It's simply absurd!" he declared and, on that indignant note, left.

I was troubled by his denial of the situation as I had spelled it out. Granted, it wasn't the easiest thing in the world to hear about oneself, but he hadn't come to supervision simply for me to throw compliments at him. He was supposed to be a professional who wanted to gain useful insight into his therapeutic practice.

During the following week, I went over and over my comments to Stan and his response, wondering whether I had come on too strong, whether I had been as bizarre and absurd as he claimed. But I couldn't see it. It was simply a case of the truth hurting like hell. And then I had a small epiphany. Maybe that's what Stan had been asking for all along, I mused. Maybe he's *wanted* me to say too much, to come down hard on him. Maybe he had been teasing me so that I would get angry at him and tell him to stop the crap and come to the point, or to stop the crap entirely. And that crap was all the sexual stuff from Samantha he had been getting a charge out of in their therapy sessions. He was feeling guilty about it and wanted me to punish him for it. Yes, I told myself, that *feels* right. It's *got* to be what's going on.

So, I ruminated further, just whom did I represent for Stan in all of this? Some important person in his life who was a thoroughgoing martinet, I imagined. His father seemed likely, especially when I recalled Stan's near reverential attitude toward our older colleague who had recommended him to me, a rigid taskmaster and harshly judgmental man. I wondered about Stan's sex life. Being a bachelor hardly precluded an active sex life in this day and age. Yet nothing in his aspect spoke of any sex life at all, outside of the jollies he was clearly getting from Samantha's follies. Although I laughed to myself at that silly phrase, I knew the situation was serious. Exploiting a patient sexually, no matter how much she might lend herself to it, is counterproductive in every respect and has no place in therapy. I half expected that Stan might cancel his next session with me. Then I realized that if I was correct in assuming that he wanted to be punished for his sexual exploitation of Samantha, he would have to return. And he did.

He was distinctly subdued that afternoon, neither meeting my eyes nor greeting me as he came in, sat down, and began to read from his notes. Their dry and sterile tone indicated that sex was to have no place in today's presentation, and I realized Stan was going to ignore the sexual issue I had raised at the conclusion of the last session. But I could not let things go on as they had been, and I interrupted him to ask where he had gotten with that issue. At first he said not far, but when I pressed him, he reluctantly agreed that there was some truth in my comments. He stopped again and it was all too plain that he was not going to help me, or himself, at all. I would have to force him to do it.

I proceeded to ask Stan how much he had discussed sex in his own therapy. With the question, he seemed to shrink within his clothes and his head bent even lower.

"Not very much," he said in a faint, almost apologetic voice.

"Don't you think that's an area you need to explore more for yourself?"

"Yes, I do," he answered faintly. Then he was silent, while I waited. Finally he lifted his head and looked straight at me. His eyes were sad and full of pain. "You know, Wayne," he continued, his voice getting louder as he went along, "what you said last week hurt me. But I thought about it and I realized you were right. I *am* a very uptight person, who lives vicariously through the lives of others."

His openness surprised me. Given the difficulty of getting him to open up at all, I had expected it would take much longer to reach this point. It was a real breakthrough. Of course, when you make an interpretation that the patient confirms, it doesn't necessarily mean you're right unless the patient's associations to it produce further supporting data, and this may happen only after a session is over and the patient is thinking back over it. In Stan's case, that data came at once, without my having to prod him as I sometimes have to do at such a point.

"I've always wished," he said, "that I could have the kinds of sexual adventures Samantha has, only they don't happen to anyone like me."

His poignant eyes and drooping mouth spoke of intense depression. But it was an emotion that transfigured his face, dispelling the aura of anachronism that had so long kept me from really feeling for him.

"What do you mean?" I asked gently.

"Look at me, Wayne!" and his gesture took in his whole length, from close-cropped head to rubber-soled shoes. "I'm not exactly the kind of guy girls go for, am I?"

"I *am* looking at you, Stan," I said, "and what I'm seeing today is something that in all the weeks you've been coming here you've never shown me—a man in pain. You've never let your real self through before. But you should. Stan. It turns you into another person, a *real* person. Someone I like a hell of a lot more than the 1950s college professor you seem determined to emulate in a sort of half-assed way!"

Stan started as I said this, and I wondered whether I had gone too far. But he only asked me, with a slightly rueful expression, where I had gotten the "1950s college professor" idea.

"Well," I answered, "I suppose it's the old-fashioned way you dress, as though you were stuck in the 1950s and the 1960s had never happened. You're sort of a walking anachronism."

Stan nodded in agreement and went on to tell me why. He said that his father had been raised in Hell's Kitchen but had managed not only to avoid all the temptations of that "caldron of sin," as he called it, but to grow up to be a professor at one of the city colleges. It was an achievement he was fiercely proud of. But even though he dressed meticulously in the prevailing style so that to look at him you could not guess his background, he had never been able to rid himself of his accent.

"And then I picked it up from him when I was little and wanted to be like him," Stan said sheepishly. "That used to drive him wild! He planned for me to be a professor like him when I grew up, and had all sorts of strict notions about my behavior and keeping myself *clean*. You know, nothing to do with smut or girls and so forth. By the time I realized he'd cut me off from other people in lots of ways, it was too late, I guess." His voice trailed off.

I let the session take this therapeutic turn because it seemed useful for Stan to talk freely now that he had begun. Speaking again, he told me that his one real rebellion was to refuse to follow his father into teaching. He had decided to be a therapist because the profession seemed to offer answers to his many questions about himself and his life. Yet now he wondered whether in the end his father's strong influence hadn't undermined the therapy he had undergone during his training. His therapist then had been an older man a lot like his father. "I never felt very free talking to him," Stan said. "I always expected him to come down on me hard as Father did."

THE DREAM OF LETTING GO

When I wondered whether he had expected me to be the same way, he said yes. Still, my being not much older than he had made it much easier to talk to me, to tell me about Samantha's sexual adventures. "I could never in the world have talked about them to my father," Stan said. "He was a total puritan and tried to raise me to be one, too, and pretty well succeeded in regard to my life if not my mind." He smiled ruefully, and went on to say what a relief and revelation it had been to him to be able to laugh with me about Samantha's exploits. "I've never had that sort of locker-room camaraderie with any man before, never dared to as a kid, for fear that my father would look at my face when I got home and somehow guess what I'd been up to. And by the time I got away from home, it was too late. It felt good to laugh with you."

He sighed heavily before he continued. "When you chewed me out about it last week, I felt deceived, as if you weren't any different from my father after all. But later, after leaving here, I thought about it and knew that you really weren't like him at all. I had to get past my feeling of hurt before I could recognize you were right."

When Stan said how much he regretted using Samantha to meet his own needs, I was able to reassure him that he hadn't harmed her irrevocably. "As a matter of fact, in a curious way," I mused aloud, "it may have allowed her to build some sort of alliance with you. Here she's regaled you week after week with all sorts of evidence of her sexuality and you haven't attempted to seduce her. I expect that in her eyes you've turned out to be a man she can trust."

"Or maybe," he said with a helpless shrug, "I'm just a eunuch in her eyes. Have you thought of that?"

Again, I reassured him, saying that however Samantha saw him in her thoughts, it was still a fantasy. "It isn't necessarily what you are in reality but what you *can* be, Stan."

When Stan left the office that day, I realized that our relationship was now firmly realistic and that I no longer perceived him as an alien presence. I was hooked by the innate humanness of his struggle. That session also had a clear and immediate effect on Stan. The following week he came in looking like, if not a new man, at least a reasonably contemporary one. A pair of blue jeans and a long-sleeved sport shirt made him look less bulky, and his aviator sunglasses were a dashing touch. He looked terrific and I told him so.

Rather than plunging into his old routine, Stan reported that in his last session with Samantha he had broached the fact that she was dealing with the sexual aspect of her life to the exclusion of everything else. Although she was at first angry and defensive, he was able to ride out the storm and get her to acknowledge the whole important area of her family and her conflicted feelings about her long estrangement from them.

"That upset her," he said, "and she cried for the first time."

I was glad to hear that, and I told him—echoing the psychiatrist at the end of *Portnoy's Complaint*—"Now the therapy can begin."

Despite Stan's change of costume and determination, as he said, not to be a walking anachronism any longer, he reported that he was still stiff in his sessions with Samantha. Eventually he decided to go back into therapy for himself so that he might deal more effectively with some of the wounds he had suffered from being his father's son. I heartily agreed with his decision. I knew that, having come to it himself, he was ready to heal and have some chance of making a real life for himself.

The therapeutic aura of our sessions together began to disappear as Stan increasingly dealt with his internal issues in his own therapy. He was at one point almost bowled over when Samantha suddenly began to experience intense sexual desire toward him and had some difficulty weathering the storm of his own arousal. With my help, he was able to master it and ultimately to help his patient confront her own inner emptiness and set her life on a positive course. By the time our supervisory sessions ended several years later, Stan had not only learned to be a good therapist but had lost a lot of weight and let his hair grow. The lean and thoughtful man who left my office for the last time had become someone I deeply respected.

After the breakthrough with Stan, I thought again about my brother and my resentful perception of him as having changed toward me. I now could see that it wasn't George who had changed but I who had passed him by. If I was disappointed in him, he was likely to be even more disappointed in himself. I called him up and we got together for the first time in many months. Talking as frankly as we had ever done, George came right out and told me that in my expecting him to measure up to a standard he had never aspired to, I had been imposing my needs on him in a way that wasn't fair to him or to our relationship. After my experience with Stan, I was ready to recognize that my brother was right. Thus I learned through him a lesson that not only brought us closer together but has stayed with me even beyond his death some years later. I hope I never forget it.

It is the simple lesson that the patient's own needs, not the therapist's, should dictate the treatment agenda. Just because you feel someone should achieve a particular goal or act in a particular way doesn't mandate that he or she should agree with you. Imposing your own wishes on another person—whether patient or supervisee or, indeed, anyone—is at best an act of indifference to his or her individuality and at worst akin to soul murder. It is a delusion to think you have the ultimate answers to all the questions that can arise in the therapeutic situation, and a therapist who thinks so needs help. This lesson is one I and every other therapist I know has to relearn every single day of our working lives. For nothing is ever final in a therapist's psyche. Shrink dreams go on forever. They are an inevitable part of the therapeutic process, and we must remain alert to their presence and their power if we are to be true healers of the minds of those who place their trust in us.

CHAPTER 7

The Dream of Overcoming Emptiness in One's Own Life

We all know of people who relive in dream and memory the horrors of some intense fear they suffered as children. That long-vanished world is too much with them, and they fight alone or through psychotherapy to subdue and master it. Then there are others, a smaller group not easily identified, who long ago banished such fears and the murderous or suicidal impulses connected with them from their inner world, at the cost of leaving it empty, airless, and even lifeless. Such people are in constant danger, since unresolved vengeful feelings have a dynamic of their own, and can seek an outlet and push those people into the web of others' anger and torment.

It is a terrible irony that someone whose life is empty in this way is resistant to psychotherapeutic help yet may well be attracted to psychiatry as a profession. This was the case with Henry. In the drive to relieve their inner tension, psychotherapists like Henry have the potential not only for victimizing patients but for endangering their very lives. However, none of these possibilities was apparent in Henry when I first met him, although he had the distinct pallor I've observed in such people. Indeed, he had the whitest, most waxen complexion of anyone I had ever seen, like the negative of a face rather than the full-color picture. I had to check myself from glancing into my office mirror to see whether he was actually reflected there.

He moved unusually slowly, his movements as languorous as some underwater plant. Rather than sitting erect, he seemed more to drape himself in the chair opposite me, his arms and legs so limp that I wondered if he would react if I stuck a pin in him. I offered him a cup of coffee and then took care to place it on the table beside him lest his languid hand let it slip and spill. And I chalked his demeanor up to poor metabolism, a lack of thyroid hormone easily remedied by a visit to an internist.

Once we began discussing his background, it was clear that Henry was a whiz at the therapeutic ropes. His training was as impeccable as the gray pin-striped three-piece suit he was wearing. A vest, I thought, on a scorcher like today! He was also wearing a gray fedora hat when he entered my office, which he had laid on the table beside him. But however much he resembled a fashion plate, he did not strike me as a dandy. He seemed rather to be *wrapped up*, letting nothing hang out, in sharp contrast to his style as a therapist in the first case he presented.

To begin with, nothing in this case forewarned me of the dangerous paths down which Henry's countertransference might lead him. I even found myself impressed by the skill with which he applied the "let it all hang out" approach to therapy. This treatment technique was based on an early theory of Freud's which encouraged patients to "discharge" their feelings so that they would not remain dammed up and lead to symptom formation. At the height of its popularity in the 1960s, it wreaked havoc on patients' mental health and on their relationships with other people. Despite my reservations about it, Henry seemed to have had a real gift for knowing just what to say and when to say it to motivate Betty, a fifty-five-year-old widow who had fallen into deep depression following her husband's recent death. After years of being the "perfect" wife and mother, with her children grown and her husband suddenly gone she felt at sea, unable to do anything but mope at home.

Henry took her apathy as a real challenge. At every session with me he would report each new step he had gotten Betty to make. She was soon well on her way to reengaging with the world she had been involved in before her husband's death. And she was opening herself up to new opportunities as well, having fun, buying extravagant clothes, redecorating her house, and reaching out of her usual circle for new friends. So expert was Henry in his interventions that I began to wonder why he was presenting Betty's case to me. If she was such a walking advertisement for the efficacy of psychotherapy, why did Henry think he needed supervision?

Then one day I began to question my admiration for Henry. The raised pitch of his voice alerted me, as I heard him repeat the time-honored declaration of rebellion, only now it was Betty who had said it and there was a twist at the end: "It's my life, and I'll live it any way I want, no matter what my children and friends say!" At that moment, I realized Henry had just told me that Betty had really kicked over the traces and had embarked on an affair with a young man less than half her age, the son of one of her oldest friends.

"You should have seen her face when she said that, Wayne," Henry remarked, a faint glow in his own face. "The image of liberation. She's getting a real kick out of shaking up her children, to say nothing of all the other people in her community who have always counted on her to be so *nice*." The last word, as he emphasized it, clearly had a rightful place in the invidious four-letter lexicon.

"Are you certain she's not slipped into a manic state?" I asked.

"I beg your pardon?" Henry's glow disappeared so fast I wondered whether my eyes had deceived me.

"It sounds as if it might be the flip side of her depression. It's not at all in keeping with her character as you've described it for her to act this way so suddenly. I wonder if you've thought about using lithium at some point?"

I had not thought Henry could get any paler. "That would be totally alien to the entire thrust of my approach," he said stiffly, almost visibly withdrawing.

I made an effort to go after him. "But you can't let Betty go on this way," I began.

"What's wrong with it?" he asked defensively. "She's made a lot of progress!"

Henry had quite a bit more to say about how Betty had been liberated from her stodgy life as wife and mother, "breaking out of the shackles of all those dull conventions and tiresome role models," as he put it, excitement again coloring his cheeks. As I listened to him, I wondered whether *I* was getting stodgy in my middle age. Could I be locking myself into the totalitarian stereotype in which a psychiatrist's first duty is to be a defender of the faith and the establishment? It was hard to knock Betty for wanting to thumb her nose at the mores that had restricted her during her previous fifty-five years of life. But *had* they restricted her? Had she truly chafed at them? Or was she, in her vulnerable state of being a new widow, responding to someone else's need as she had responded to the needs of her family over the years?

No, I thought, this affair with her friend's son was probably quite inappropriate, to say nothing of Betty's recent financial extravagances in buying an expensive new wardrobe and in totally refurnishing her house, which I now saw in an entirely new light. Her behavior was clearly overturning values in respect to responsibility and sexuality which she had cherished all her life. Also, her newfound "freedom" was all too likely to make her a pariah in her community. I doubted whether after a lifetime of depending on husband, family, and friends she had the inner resources to sustain that freedom. It seemed to me that hers was too rapid and global a change to be merely the result of the sort of flowering of inner potential we hope for in a successful psychotherapy. The seduction of this young man would be more than just a "healthy fling"; it would be self-destructive for her and likely hurt him as well.

THE DREAM OF OVERCOMING EMPTINESS

I kept my thoughts to myself as Henry reached the conclusion of his peroration: "A new life is opening up for Betty, a life of freedom and self-expression she never even dreamed of before!" His eyes were positively glittering in that moon-pale face, and his fingers trembling as they fiddled with a vest button.

Freedom! An alluring word that evokes a state we all feel deprived of, all yearn for. Yet real freedom has to be of our own making, out of our own needs—not imposed upon us by others for their needs. I now suspected that Henry was unconsciously attempting to do that with Betty, and if she was allowed to pursue the course she was taking, she could cause untold damage to her own life as well as to that of the young man. But this was not the moment to confront Henry on his share in Betty's crisis. The issue was to get her out of it and, choosing my words carefully, I explained what I saw as dangerous in Betty's behavior. As Henry listened to me, he neither nodded nor in any other way indicated that he accepted or understood my comments. His polite reserve bespoke silent criticism. When I finished, he said nothing for some minutes.

"Well, Wayne," he began at last, clearly forcing out the words. "I can't say I buy your argument. But how about if I arrange for Betty to have a consultation with a psychopharmacologist, and then we can decide whether to use drugs?'"

With more animation than usual, he assembled himself in a standing position, picked up his hat, nodded curtly, and left.

While comfortable with the resolution Henry had suggested, I was not comfortable with his apparent disdain of my arguments. Was ours simply a difference of opinion and personality, or a sign of an inner difficulty of his own we needed to examine? His manner made me no wiser when he told me two weeks later that a psychopharmacologist had pronounced Betty to be in a manic state and that the lithium he had prescribed was helping her significantly. When I asked Henry how he felt about that, he said with his usual cool composure,

"Well, I sure did goof in not picking up on the mania." The faint shrug of one gray pin-striped shoulder dismissed further discussion.

I went along with the signal, deciding not to take him to task about his part in encouraging Betty in her rebellion. He had been punished enough by having his judgment counter-manded by the psychopharmacologist. And recalling my own "goofs" as a fledgling psychiatrist, I felt that Henry couldn't help but see this as an occasion for serious self-examination. And anyway, we had retrieved Betty in time. No one had been hurt.

Henry's next case was very different. Vincent, an anesthe-siologist in his early thirties, had recently come to Henry for help with serious attacks of anxiety. "And the worst of it is," said Henry, although I sensed that in some way it might be for him the "best," "is these attacks come over Vincent when he's administering anesthesia to a patient on the operating table!"

Clearly a perilous situation. But again, I had to admire Hen-ry's initial command of the case, his ingenuity in helping Vin-cent avert the moments of panic that threatened to unnerve him during an operation, moments when a wrong move or lapse in attention could mean a patient's life. I was also im-pressed by Henry's patience. It is a quality that serves a ther-apist well in freeing a relatively buttoned-up patient as Vincent was, enabling him to open himself up in accord with his own internal timetable and not because of outside pres-sure from the therapist. That opening up did seem long in coming, however. Our sessions began to appear like exercises in suspense, as Henry would recount a particularly serious operation where Vincent had come within a hair's breadth of flipping out, only to be saved in the nick of time by recalling a suggestion of Henry's. And I noticed that woven through each account was a sort of minor theme having to do with Vincent's anger at the incompetence of various surgeons.

After one such session, I felt a downward tug of exhaustion as Henry closed the door behind him. This was getting tire-some, and I knew my weariness was a sign, not of a long day or a late night, but of the fact that there was no real engagement between Henry and me. We were on a treadmill getting nowhere fast, although I wondered how long Vincent could keep on holding off his panic, whether something in him that wanted to botch an operation and kill a patient might not get the upper hand in spite of Henry's clever interventions. Were Vincent and Henry trying to resolve a problem or were they collaborators in building up to a disaster?

So far Henry had not managed to unearth an ounce of insight into the reason for Vincent's attacks. Apparently it had nothing to do with his wife and baby daughter, whom he dearly loved. Nor was it lack of money. So there had to be something in Vincent's past relationships with his family to account for his dangerous state. I realized I would have to activate Henry if we were to help Vincent in a deeper way before he did someone irretrievable harm.

At the next session, rather than waiting for Henry to begin, I pointed out to him that in all these weeks he hadn't given me any idea of what Vincent was really like. "What does he look like, for example?"

"Well, he's as tall as I am, well over six feet, but really heavy. He overshadows all the surgeons at his hospital." Henry paused, then added in the oddest tone, like a little brother about a big one. "There's not much he's afraid of."

"Bravo, Henry!" I said, in a conscious attempt to repress my irritation at having to drag information out of him. "That's the most definite thing you've said about Vincent in the four sessions you've been talking about him!"

As I spoke, I was aware of feeling testy toward Henry, even that he had been consciously withholding information from me. At the same time, I wondered whether I was being defensive and maligning him in order to cover over my recent failure to realize that we were in a rut. However we had gotten into it, it was a rut and my immediate task was to get Henry out of it. I realized that Henry had indeed been holding out on me in not supplying the basic data about Vincent's family background. And, diverted by the drama of the almost-disasters Henry had been reporting, I hadn't asked about it. I asked now.

Like most psychotherapists listening to a supervisee or a patient, I allow the data to float freely in a part of my mind until they are ready to connect. The assumption is that they will ultimately compose into a consistent scenario that explains most of the problems of the life I am examining. Now at last Henry began to give me information about Vincent's life that promised to give us such a scenario.

Vincent had grown up in an upstate town in which his father had been a leading light, a respected general practitioner who also functioned as the only surgeon. When Vincent was about twelve, things changed drastically. The community was thriving, and as a token of its success built a good-sized hospital which wanted on its staff a board-qualified surgeon, not a physician like his father. The loss of surgical work significantly reduced both the family's income and its status. It also embittered Vincent's father, who became morose and withdrawn. The boy used to dream of growing up and being a doctor himself—and having his own hospital where he could install his father as chief surgeon. More realistically, he looked forward to being able eventually to get closer to his father and talk to him about what had happened, as neither his mother nor his father ever openly discussed the situation in front of him. That day never came. Just before he went off to college, his father was admitted to the hospital for what should have been a routine gallbladder operation. But the surgeon botched it somehow, and Vincent's father died on the operating table.

"Ah!" I said, sensing the key to Vincent's trouble. "How did the boy take his father's death?"

"He was upset and furious because his mother just took it lying down," Henry said, his voice charged with indignation, almost as if it has been *his* mother.

"What do you mean?"

"He wanted her to sue the surgeon who had done the gallbladder operation, but she squelched him, saying that it wasn't proper for a doctor's family to try to destroy the reputation of another physician. And Vincent was too young to take matters into his own hands." Again, Henry looked as if he, too, was a Saint George not yet old enough to wield the heavy sword required to slay the dragon.

As I pondered the fact that Vincent had not only chosen to be a doctor himself but was spending each and every working day of his life playing a subordinate role to a company of surgeons, I recalled the theme threading through all of Henry's accounts of Vincent's irritation at the surgeons. Might that not be more than a minor theme, but rather the leitmotif of his life? Might he not be working each day with a group of surgeons because, in fueling his anger toward the one who had caused his father's death, it offered him some belated way of attempting to master the original trauma and the painful feelings that followed? And what if that attempt was somehow thwarted? Wouldn't an anxiety attack be an almost inevitable consequence of such a scenario? It sounded reasonable, I thought, and decided it was worthwhile interrupting Henry to ask him what he thought was bothering Vincent.

"Oh," Henry replied casually, "just the thing he's been having with one of the bigwigs on the medical staff of the hospital."

"What kind of thing?" I pursued, in spite of Henry's obvious reluctance to talk about it.

"The man's simply incompetent," he said, with all the assurance of those who had once burned anyone at the stake for claiming the earth went around the sun.

"How do you know?" I asked.

"It's obvious! Everyone knows, Vincent says." Henry was getting exercised, his cheeks pink and his eyes flashing. Somehow or other, I was pressing him where it hurt.

"Beyond the issue of this fellow's competence in the here and now," I said quietly, hoping to calm Henry down and keep on the track of our main problem, "is how Vincent's anger connects to the episode in his past you've been telling me about."

"You mean the surgeon who screwed up on his father?"

I nodded, not knowing whether Henry had understood this connection all along. When he left that day, I felt that he was stirred up as never before. I hoped that it meant he would use this insight to give Vincent some real relief. How could he have missed the obvious importance of this connection?

The following week, to my dismay, Henry marched in with unaccustomed vigor and announced, "Vincent's anger's out now! The chief of surgery is really going to get it!"

Henry's cheeks were flushed as I hadn't seen them since the days he was bringing me a new, enthralling installment of Betty's indiscretions. But I merely asked, "What's up?"

"He says the man's got to be an alcoholic. The chief's hands shake when he operates, particularly after a weekend or holiday. Last Monday he nicked a major artery in an elderly male patient without even noticing, and they had to give the man a few extra units of blood in order to keep his pressure up. Vincent said he felt absolutely livid when the operation was over but no one was willing to say a word about it."

"Sure does echo what happened with his father, doesn't it?"

"When I asked him about that, he really blew up! It took him ten or fifteen minutes to cool down." And as he told me this, Henry's face was alive with energy, reflecting Vincent's fiery anger. I was certain now that the two men both needed the stimulus of others to make themselves and their anger come alive.

"Do we know anything about the man who operated on *Vincent's* father? Was *he* an alcoholic?"

"When Vincent asks his mother about that, she puts him off," Henry said. "Tells him to stop dwelling in the past."

"She's right, of course," I said, but sensing that Henry was trying to avoid my question, I added, "except that it's still the raging, painful present as far as he's concerned. Not until he can let go of it will it be really in the past."

Henry's "Yes" sounded more as if he was echoing me rather than speaking out of real conviction.

"By the way," I shifted to a point that had been bothering

me since Henry's first words that day, "you didn't tell me at our last session that the bigwig Vincent is upset with is the chief of surgery. That's a pretty powerful dragon to take on."

"Sure is, isn't it? You really have to hand it to him!"

"You may, Henry, but I don't," I cut in more sternly than I usually do with anyone, supervisee or patient. But, recalling Betty's case and its potential for disaster, I felt a warning was in order. "Don't push Vincent. Remember, Henry, it's *his* life and *his* anger. He needs to be certain that what he's expressing in the present is right for that present and not some relic of the past. Nowadays we don't go after our enemies with broadswords. We try to contain ourselves a bit, in order to defuse or understand a dangerous situation before it gets out of hand."

Henry's response was wholly involuntary. All the color left his face, as if blasted out by a high wind. Then he buttoned up his jacket and looked at me in the way he had of not seeming to see me or to be taking anything in. As I looked back at him, I once again had that chill sense of emptiness and incorporeality. It stayed with me, disquietingly, for a long time after he had left. If I did not know better, I would have thought he was all skeleton, neither flesh nor muscle nor nerves to hold him together. No way to be glad. No way to be unhappy.

I worried about Vincent as well. I didn't like the idea of that big burly fellow regulating the rate of anesthetic flow during some poor patient's surgery, feeling that only by throwing his weight around in some drastic way could he get over the fury and the helplessness he had felt at his father's death. But there was nothing I could do directly. My only approach to him was through Henry.

It's always chastening to have one's hopes for the best dashed, as mine were at the next session. "Vincent's done it!" Henry proclaimed from the doorway, his flushed cheeks an all-too-clear indication that excitement was on the boil. "He's planning to bring the chief of surgery up before the medical board of the hospital!"

Psychiatrists get pretty hardened to hearing all sorts of bad news, but at this I was appalled. No one but a fool takes on the chief of a medical department, unless he has an ironclad case. "What's the charge?" I asked.

"Incompetence," Henry said, sitting down in the chair, his air of complacency bringing into sharp focus his usual ethereal self.

"You can't be serious!"

But Henry was not a joking type. All along his inability to respond to the humor that I depend on to help build rapport with a supervisee or a patient had somewhat irritated me. It was another of the roadblocks he put in the way of real understanding.

Henry went on to report that on the previous weekend the two of them, Vincent and the chief of surgery, had both been preparing for an emergency operation. "The chief was loaded—"

"How do you know?" I couldn't help but interrupt.

"Vincent said he was, of course," Henry replied, as if speaking of the source of ultimate truth.

"Of course," I echoed. I motioned him to go on, seeing him impervious to my irony.

"The operation didn't go well. A lot of unnecessary blood loss again. Vincent says that if one of the residents hadn't acted to save him, the patient would have died on the table. And afterward in the doctors' locker room, Vincent chewed out the chief in front of everyone and then stormed out before anyone could say a word. He plans to present the preliminary charges any day now."

Henry sat back then, his eyes hardly seeing me in their preoccupation with some inner vision. He hadn't spoken so fervently or looked so intense since our argument about Betty and her inappropriate behavior. I had no need to ask him where he stood in respect to Vincent's action. He was all too clearly 100 percent behind his patient. I knew that if I had any hope of getting Henry to see the dangerous position he had allowed that patient to get into, I would have to tread carefully. Antagonizing Henry would be totally counterproductive.

"Loyalty's a great quality," I began, "and it's clear you feel it strongly. I like that. But there's a problem with it."

Already Henry was stiffening, retiring into his "retreat" mode. I had no choice but to go on if I was to help him and avoid disaster for Vincent. "The problem with loyalty for a psychotherapist is that if you allow yourself to feel 'my patient right or wrong' it can cloud your judgment about what is really going on with that person. In the case of Vincent, by preventing him from understanding his youthful anger, you're making it impossible for him to learn to master it. You're depriving him of any real freedom of choice. You're sentencing him to remain entrapped in his old anger, with all its dangers for him and for others."

Henry almost levitated out of his chair, his cheeks positively ruddy. "Are you questioning my support of Vincent?" he sputtered.

I was startled by his quick spring to the attack. Although one purpose of our sessions was to call his judgment into question when necessary, his response was unusually defensive, as if by casting doubt on him I had touched a raw nerve.

"Has it occurred to you, Henry," I asked, hoping to connect with him in this rare moment of animation, "that you treat every issue that comes up between us as an all-or-none question of your competence as a psychotherapist?"

"But you're questioning what I did!"

"Sure I am," I acknowledged. "But that's not really the issue, is it? Let's concentrate on Vincent, on what he's doing or is about to do. Tell me, is anyone who was in that operating room willing to corroborate his story about the chief's being drunk?"

"What does that matter? He *saw* the man was loaded. Isn't that enough?"

"Come on, Henry!" I said, irritation creeping into my voice at his pigheadedness. "This is the real world! Since when does a staff peon attempt to indict the chief of surgery without being backed up by the testimony of at least a dozen witnesses?"

Henry was shaking his head, as if my words were a swarm of hornets he was trying to get free of. "You're doing the same thing you did with Betty, Wayne."

"Meaning?"

"Coming down on the side of the establishment. That side of your personality is really hard for me to take." His cheeks were filled with color now, and his expression more definite than it had ever been before. It was as if he had drawn sustenance from somewhere.

From me, dammit! I thought ruefully.

Of course, I could have pointed out that he, too, was doing the same thing he had done in Betty's case, coming down on the opposite side. But it's never useful to get in the game of charge and countercharge. Besides, that would be playing into Henry's hands. He wanted to provoke me to anger, to get me to lose control of myself. It was as if he, like Vincent, needed to feel raped and put upon by the establishment—needed it so much, in fact, as to create conditions under which the establishment had no choice but to come down hard on him.

"Henry," I said, reaching for calmness, "I'm not exactly sure what you want to accomplish right now. But if you're trying to portray me as some sort of spineless creep who wants to cover up a doctor's negligence, it's irrelevant to the main issue. What matters right now is that your unquestioning encouragement of Vincent's actions could ruin his career and his life. Tell me, Henry, where is that self-righteousness going to get you, or more important, Vincent, when he fails to convince the medical board of his charges? And that's more than likely to happen if all he's got going for him is his uncorroborated word. That will put a big black mark on his record. What will he do with that? How will he live with it? How can you be sure he's acting out of a real situation and not displacing onto the chief of surgery his rage against the doctor who botched his father's operation? Tell me, Henry, how can you justify the stand you've taken?"

By the time I had finished, Henry was hopping with anger, starting out of his chair as if each word was pricking him.

"Dammit, Wayne!" he shouted. "I'm not on trial. The chief of surgery is."

Mentally I threw up my hands at Henry's obtuseness, but said only "Whoever's on trial, it's my guess that it will be Vincent, neither you nor the chief, who will be found guilty. And it will be Vincent who suffers the sentence."

When Henry left shortly afterward, the anger I had been suppressing came to the surface. He had been attempting to provoke me, and he had succeeded. But thank goodness, I hadn't played into his hands entirely and let him see it as strongly as I felt it. I hadn't let him draw all the blood he yearned for to enliven his impoverished psyche. I wasn't especially surprised when the following week he left a message on my answering machine to cancel our session. As a matter of fact, it wouldn't have surprised me if he decided to terminate the supervision entirely at that point. But I had a sneaking suspicion he still thought he could provoke my anger in order to justify the existence of his own.

Henry did show up the next week. His skin wasn't strikingly pale and he seemed detached rather than belligerent or retiring. Irritated as I still felt, I knew that unleashing a barrage of angry interpretations would be as counterproductive as it had seemed two weeks before. Prudence required me to sit back in my chair and wait for him to make the first move.

"Look, Wayne," he began, "I canceled last week because I didn't want to talk to you. But much as I dislike acknowledging it to you, I need help with Vincent. The preliminary hearing was a disaster for him, and now the medical board is zeroing in on his outburst in the locker room. There's a big chance he'll get sacked and end up before the ethics committee of the county medical society. I'm not saying I have any responsibility for his getting into this fix, but I want to help him and haven't any idea how. Do you?"

I was relieved that Henry wanted to take action even if he couldn't accept his role in the situation. In response to his plea, I suggested that he offer to testify before the board in person or through a deposition.

"And what would I say?"

"You'd explain about Vincent's father's death and how Vincent's therapy has mobilized an immense amount of unresolved anger from the past toward the doctor responsible for it. Then you'd go on to describe how this rage got displaced in the here and now onto the persona of the chief of surgery. In that way, the board might see its way clear to making psychotherapy, rather than Vincent himself, the scapegoat for his aberrant behavior."

"Will it save his job, do you think?"

"There's no telling. But if that's the only thing he loses, he'll be lucky. He'll be able to find another job without much trouble, and then he can go about the business of trying to get his life back on track."

"And if I don't decide to sell out the stand he's taken?" Henry's chin was jutting forward. I'd never seen him so lively.

"Then you're selling *him* out," I snapped back. "You might as well give him the gun to blow his brains out at once."

I regretted the words the moment they were out of my mouth. I hadn't meant to be so harsh. Or had I?

Henry stared at me for a moment. Then a rare smile flashed across his face. "You don't like me, do you?" It was more a statement than a question.

"I don't like the way you operate, Henry," I said flatly. "You create Sturm und Drang in other people's lives to jazz up your own, and the worst of it is that those people are coming to you for help and relying on you to give it. You're obligated at the very least not to use them or to make their troubles worse. As for my not liking you, you haven't allowed me to know you well enough to find out. But whether I do or not is beside the point. The point is to help Vincent out of the predicament you've encouraged him to get into. It strikes me that far from helping him with his anxiety in respect to a small area of his life, you've given him real cause to be anxious about all of it."

In the end, Henry took my advice and was allowed to testify before the medical board's investigating committee. As he reported his testimony to me, it sounded angry and defiant.

Nonetheless he managed to function successfully as Vincent's advocate. The upshot was that the young anesthesiologist was allowed to resign his position at the hospital without any blot on his record. He quickly got a new job in another city, and there was referred to another psychiatrist.

At the session when Henry reported this hopeful conclusion to Vincent's story, I decided it was time to see whether my supervisee and I could get on a more productive footing. I dispensed with the niceties and cut right through to the heart of the matter. "Henry, I told you recently that I don't like the way you operate, creating havoc in other people's lives to fill the emptiness in your own. My guess is that your parents or some other important person in your early life hurt you a hell of a lot and your way of dealing with your anger and rebelliousness has been to wall yourself off from them. But that doesn't mean they're dead. They are all too much alive, and to cope with them you alternate between playing possum and being an agent provocateur. You're so out of touch with your own dangerous feelings that I wonder whether that isn't what inspired you to become a therapist, just to satisfy your need to spur others on to act out those feelings for you. Because then, and only then, *can* you feel. It's a poor show, Henry. A lousy way to live and even lousier to be in a position of power, egging others on to fulfill your own needs! My recommendation to you is get yourself some psychotherapy before you hurt anyone else!"

My words were harsh, but there was a part of Henry, I knew, that wanted to accept their truth. Instead he withdrew, growing paler and paler, as if all the blood in his body was draining away, making his fury as invisible from himself as from me. When I was finished, he was farther from me than ever. It did not take the deliberate way he put his fedora on his head to tell me I had not reached him. His face was eloquent. His eyes, although still on me, were totally blank, and his mouth clamshell-tight, the line of lip barely visible. He got up and left, closing the door behind him without a sound.

I was sorry—not to lose him as a supervisee so much as to

have been unable to help him. There are, I am happy to say, relatively few people who seek to fill the emptiness in their lives by stirring up others and even fewer of these who are psychiatrists. It is the nature of this disturbance to be hard to treat. I believed that Henry had come to me in the first place because in the healthy part of himself he had some faint glimmering that he was not doing right by his patients. But beyond that, it had been too painful for him to go. When he left my office for the last time, I had the chilling thought that he had learned nothing. And that in all probability, neither I nor anyone else could stop him from continuing to wreak havoc in the lives of the troubled men and women who counted on him to help them.

CHAPTER 8

The Dream of Having the Perfect Child

W hen a baby is born, it's almost never a stranger to its parents, since they have had nine months to create the child in their minds. In the new arrival, parents see a way of renewing old relationships, fulfilling missed opportunities, and repairing their own imperfections. In short, they harbor the dream of having the perfect child.

In the same manner, a therapist can dream of turning a patient into a perfect child. When this happens, it's usually an effort to create a better version of the therapist or of the therapist's own children. I once supervised a therapist, however, who dreamed of the perfect child but not for the usual reasons. The real reason, in fact, was buried so deep in her unconscious that it constituted a major mystery.

I had known Terry for several years before she asked for my help. In the local chapter of our professional association, she was a "fixture," and I use that word as a compliment. She had been the secretary of a committee on which I also served, holding the group together in a motherly fashion, smoothing differences among political factions, taking care of nitpicking details, and mentoring younger members. Yet she had also found time to write articles and even a book. Sometimes I felt a touch of envy at Terry's ability to keep so many balls in the air at once. I admired her too, particularly for her no-nonsense approach to life. Once, while chairing a meeting, she told a self-important psychiatrist who had gone on way too long that what he was saying made no sense at all. So I was flattered to learn that Terry admired me for being straightforward, too.

"I'm asking for your supervision, Wayne, because I need someone who won't bullshit me," she said at our first meeting. As if to emphasize the point, Terry leaned forward and looked me right in the eye. She was having trouble, she said, with a young patient, Molly van der Cleer, a third-year student at the same medical school Terry herself had attended. Molly had been referred to her by an old friend who knew Molly's family well.

When I asked Terry to define her problem with Molly, she called it "an attack of dumbness." "I'm not acting like myself," she went on. "Would you believe, I'm insisting that she stay in medical school, even though she came to me because she's not sure that's what she wants to do. I come down on her real hard sometimes, as if I'm going to throttle her. Frankly, it scares me."

Straight from the shoulder, or so it seemed. I took a moment to scrutinize Terry's appearance. Although I had not seen her for over a year, she looked just the same: classic suit, "sensible" shoes, pageboy hairdo, a modicum of makeup. She wore no rings on either hand and no other jewelry besides a workmanlike digital watch. Just your basic, no-frills therapist, her ensemble seemed to say. The only change I noticed in Terry was the increased amount of gray in her hair. Perhaps she didn't trouble to dye it because she felt totally comfortable with herself. Or maybe she thought that taking a few years off her age, which seemed to be fiftyish, would have constituted "bullshitting."

But even with artifice eschewed, Terry was attractive enough. She had an open face—clear complexion, bright eyes, full mouth—and a tall and trim, if somewhat angular, figure. Her hands were large and strong, the type of hands that could have held the reins of a covered wagon heading west. In spite of her professional outfit, she had the stalwart looks of a pioneer woman.

Terry noticed that I was evaluating her. "If I look like a pretty strong character, Wayne, it's because I am. It was a struggle for me to become a doctor. Nobody handed me anything on a silver platter. Maybe that's why I'm being so tough on Molly, but honestly . . ."

Terry told me about her background, in which there was nothing that indicated she might wind up in medicine. Hers was a blue-collar family in a factory town in Massachusetts. Just about everyone in town worked in the factory, and Terry's father was no exception. But when Terry was nine years old, an accident at the factory left her father crippled. After that, he stayed home, ruminating on his injury and becoming increasingly passive. Terry's mother went to work, leaving Terry and her two younger brothers with an embittered, noncommunicative father.

Young as she was, Terry took on much of the child care. She found that she liked "playing mother." What pained her was the deteriorating relationship between her parents. Her mother became increasingly angry at her father's "helplessness." She accused him of malingering. She often screamed at him, and if he tried to answer back, she would throw things. Terry felt sorry for her father. His enforced passivity seemed to increase her love for him. As for her mother, Terry steered clear of her as much as possible, since she constantly criticized Terry, too.

Terry described her adolescence as "stormy." She would have been "down the tubes," she said, had it not been for the intervention of a beloved science teacher who, impressed by the girl's spunk, encouraged her to aim higher than the factory. She helped Terry get a scholarship to the nursing school of a Boston hospital. Terry's mother was vehemently opposed to the idea. She told Terry she wasn't smart enough. She accused her of running out on the family. But Terry persevered. Not only did she not flunk out of nursing school, she did brilliantly. Her self-confidence soared. After she got her first nursing job, she started sending money home, a practice she continued to this day. But even so, her mother never forgave her.

After a few years in nursing, Terry told me she began to think about becoming a doctor. "I wanted to be in charge, Wayne," she explained. "I realized I was as smart as those doctors. There was one intern—if I hadn't told him what to do, he would have killed a patient. I got tired of holding doctors' hands and seeing them get all the glory."

Terry was accepted by a major medical school in New York City. It turned out to be a wonderful experience, in spite of the long hours, the fatigue, and the fear of never being able to pay off the money she had to borrow for her expenses. Terry fell in love with medicine. She found it to be "the one thing that's never let me down."

"And something—or someone—else did?" I asked, taking the bait.

The "someone" was a fellow student in medical school with whom Terry had had a passionate affair. "There isn't much to tell," she commented guardedly. "It was, and then it wasn't. And even though it ended twenty-five years ago, there hasn't been anyone serious since."

Terry went on to say that she had had some therapy of her own, which ended prematurely because of her therapist's death. She had little to report about the treatment, except for the fact that it had been valuable. Then she moved on to the reason she had come for supervision: Molly van der Cleer, the patient who was having second thoughts about pursuing a medical career. In Molly's case, such thoughts were highly inconvenient. Since the mid-nineteenth century, there had been at least one medical person in each generation of her family. A van der Cleer, currently represented in the person of Molly's grandmother, always served on the board of the hospital whose medical school Molly attended. And Molly's father, Charles van der Cleer, was a successful surgeon with a society practice. Recently, Terry noted, he had received some award or other from a professional association.

"It must be a hard act for Molly to follow," I commented.

Terry seemed a trifle surprised. "Maybe," she said, "but I'm sure she's up to it. And her situation has many advantages. It doesn't hurt, in any field, to have family connections." Even without her "connections," Terry believed, Molly could have gotten into medical school. She was a Phi Beta Kappa graduate of an Ivy League college, and she had an excellent background in science. She was a "natural" for medicine, Terry commented.

Why, then, was Molly having doubts?

Molly had told Terry she thought she might not belong in medical school because she was "screwing up." The "screwups," however, sounded minor the way Terry described them to me. Molly had rung up a C or two on exams, and in a few instances she had "drifted off" in class and found everyone staring at her when the instructor asked her a question. In Molly's mind, the daydreaming meant she wasn't really interested in medicine.

But daydreaming, if it doesn't happen constantly, is normal enough, I thought. In Molly's case it could have been a defense against anxiety—perhaps the instructor was talking about a subject that frightened her—or she could have been using it as a means of reworking an earlier traumatic experience. I would have expected Terry to question Molly about her "screwups" and go on to explore the reasons for her qualms about medical school. Molly's expectations of herself might be too high. Or she might need some time off. Then again, perhaps medicine was really boring her, and she would be better suited to another profession.

But there was something in Terry's expression that let me know Molly's career choice wasn't something to be explored; it was something to be confirmed. Her next statement made that clear. "I know the 'screwups' are minor, Wayne. Yet that's not what I told Molly. I accused her of engaging in self-sabotage, of trying to botch things up. I insisted that she see me more frequently, because something really serious was going on. I frightened her so much, she agreed to it. I can't believe how dictatorial I was. It's almost as if the words were coming out of someone else's mouth."

Terry looked truly distressed, which was a good sign. All too often, I have found, a therapist does not realize when his or her behavior may be harmful to a patient. Terry did. "You came down on her like a parent, an angry desperate parent," I said. "I wonder why it's so important to you that Molly become a doctor."

"Because I know she really wants to be one."

"Even though she says she's not sure."

"Yes."

I told Terry what she well knew, that her insistence on behaving like a parent, and not a very understanding one at that, indicated a countertransference blind spot. We needed to find out the reasons for her strong feelings, or at least keep them from affecting her patient. The blind spot, I pointed out, had caused Terry to come to a "premature closure" in her treatment of Molly. Way before all the evidence was in, she had decided that Molly should stick to her original career goal. Yet Molly had discussed other interests, of which writing was a primary one. In college, she had edited the literary magazine, and she had considered getting a master's degree in writing instead of going to medical school. It had been a difficult choice, and now Molly wondered if she had made the right one.

Terry, however, dismissed Molly's writing out of hand. She felt an intense need to have her stay in medical school. I wondered what could explain the extraordinary pressure Terry was putting on Molly. And it occurred to me that Terry was as determined to keep Molly in a professional school as her own mother had been determined to keep Terry out of one.

Terry must have been very angry at her mother's attitude, and I thought she might be trying to give Molly the encouragement she wished she had had. But instead of being supportive, Terry was acting in a dictatorial fashion, just like her mother. That would explain Terry's statement that the words she had used with Molly "seemed to be coming out of someone else's mouth."

This idea intrigued Terry. She knew she was still resentful toward her mother, and she knew she was taking a parental attitude toward Molly, but it hadn't occurred to her to put the two things together. We were off to a good start on the supervisory process, which in the weeks ahead would consist of listening to Terry, evaluating what she was doing, offering suggestions, and just plain hanging in there. I mentioned to Terry that the next time she felt like being "dictatorial" toward Molly, she might keep silent, step back, and evaluate her own emotions. A new set of associations would emerge. They might resonate with Terry's mother, or they might be related to feelings Molly was unconsciously setting up in Terry. By examining those associations, we would explore why Terry had a need to come down "hard" on Molly. As for me, I planned to be "hard" on Terry, I said, "because I know you don't want any bullshit."

"Will I live to regret this?" But Terry smiled as she asked the question. She was relieved, she confided, to know that someone else was "on the case." As she walked out of my office, I noticed an increased buoyancy in her stride.

I was glad that Terry felt confidence in me, but I was left with a nagging thought. Why hadn't this "dictatorial" problem come up before in Terry's career? She had been treating patients for a long time, and had probably encountered other women medical students. She had mentored many residents and was known for her supportive and nonjudgmental style. There had to be something very special about Molly—or the van der Cleers—that was setting Terry off. I suspected that finding out what it was wouldn't be easy.

A few days later, I was leafing through a medical newspaper when I spotted a photograph of Charles van der Cleer receiving the award Terry had mentioned. He was seated on a dais, his arms folded across his chest, with several empty chairs next to him. Apparently, some of the other award recipients had failed to show up. As a result, the photo had an element of sadness about it—a striking picture of an isolated man. I looked at it for a moment, then put it out of my mind, or so I thought.

At our next session, Terry reported that she had followed my suggestion about "stepping back." Molly told her about an examination she had barely managed to pass. Instead of studying "as hard as usual," she had been busy writing a short story. The thought of writing a story when an exam was coming up was anathema to Terry. She wanted to tell Molly that she must stop sabotaging herself in this way. Instead, she kept quiet and waited.

"The image of my mother came into my mind," Terry recalled. "I saw her storming in the door at six o'clock and accusing me of not getting dinner started. She was always on my case, as if she had to show me the error of my ways. I guess that's what I feel I have to do for Molly."

"You want to give Molly a medical career so badly, you're even following a role model you know was poor," I commented. "But it's good that you were able to resist lecturing her about staying in school. Since she comes from a medical dynasty, I suspect that someone in the family is already putting on pressure. Any idea who it might be?"

Terry thought for a minute. "Probably Helene van der Cleer, her mother, if you can call her that."

Terry seemed to be upset by the mere thought of Helene, whom she described as cold and indifferent. "She's your classic narcissist, interested only in herself," Terry said. "Helene can't suspend her own needs long enough to do anything for anybody else, which is what mothering takes. She has to be the center of attention all the time."

Terry told me what Molly had told her about her mother. Soon after Molly's birth, Helene had decided to devote herself to what she termed her "calling," writing. But she couldn't do it in the family's Park Avenue apartment, where she could also have given her only child some attention. Instead, she had the caretaker's cottage on the family's Connecticut estate remodeled into an office, and she spent her time there. On weekends, when the family joined her, she held "readings," during which everyone, including Molly as soon as she grew old enough to understand language, was expected to comment favorably on her efforts. If Molly expressed delight, she got hugs and kisses, for a short time. Then it was back to New York, where she was cared for by a succession of nannies, while Helene remained in Connecticut. For Molly, Helene shone "like a distant star," to use Winston Churchill's words about his frequently absent mother.

Needless to say, the relationship between Molly's parents was absent, too. As Molly described it to Terry, even in their limited time together they kept their distance. They were polite enough, but there was a dangerous edge to their politeness, as if they wanted to use angry words instead of nice ones. It made Molly sad and uncomfortable too, she said. She would have preferred having equal time alone with each of them, but the practical fact was that the only one who made time for her was her father.

Helene became even busier after she obtained some recognition for her esoteric novels and went on the college lecture circuit. "I'm not knocking her success, Wayne," Terry told me. "You know that I approve of women being committed to their careers. It's just that Helene's done it in such an extreme way. Molly's always realized that she rates a poor second to Helene's writing, yet writing is an interest she shares with her mother."

Terry had concluded that for Molly writing was a way of gaining maternal approval, rather than something she actually enjoyed. It was a red herring, she thought, in terms of career choice, although she had never bothered to explore this idea with Molly. Another instance of premature closure, I thought. There was something else, too. As I listened to Terry's recitation, I realized it was informative but out of kilter. I had asked who might be pressuring Molly to stay in medical school. Instead, she had told me about Helene van der Cleer who, damaging as she sounded, wasn't "coming down hard" on Molly about medicine.

Terry was deliberately missing the point. "What about her dad, the award-winning surgeon?" I asked. "Doesn't he want her to become a doctor?"

"Of course he does," Terry replied. "But he hasn't had to pressure her. With Helene out of the picture so much of the time, he and Molly have been unusually close. Even as a little girl, she shared his interest in medicine. He'd take her to the hospital and explain all of the equipment in the laboratory. She remembers it with real pleasure. It was all very natural."

In Terry's view, the doctor had been a fine parent, considering the demands of his own career and the stresses of his "rotten" marital situation. Helene wasn't always alone in Connecticut, Terry confided. A number of prominent men visited her there regularly, and this was known to everyone in the van der Cleer circle. Terry got this information from Charles's old friend who had referred Molly to her. Charles van der Cleer, she had concluded, was a wronged man.

It was natural for a friend to see things from Charles's point of view. But a therapist should be more interested in putting things in perspective. True, Helene sounded like a less than ideal mother, but Charles had been pretty weak, too. Why had he concurred in a marital arrangement that was so bad for his child? And, even more important, why was Terry so anxious to defend him?

"I'm not defending him," Terry replied in an acerbic tone, when I put the question to her.

"That doesn't sound like my no-bullshit Terry."

"Really, Wayne, this is making me upset." Terry began breathing in and out rapidly, so rapidly that she was in danger of hyperventilating. She put her hands on her knees to steady herself. Then she got up, walked to the window, leaned on the air conditioner, and stared at the wall of the building opposite my office. After a minute or so, she was breathing normally again.

As she returned to the chair, she smiled at me. "I didn't mean to get defensive, Wayne," she said.

"And I didn't mean to push too hard."

Terry seemed relieved. I could see it was best to avoid the subject of Charles van der Cleer for a while. Besides, our time was up for the day.

I was surprised, however, to see that Terry could become disturbed so easily. Clearly, she was not as composed as she appeared to be. Beneath her no-nonsense attitude there was another Terry, the guardian of a secret. Would I ever get to know that Terry? Only by closely following her treatment of Molly could I hope to find the answer.

At our next session, I asked Terry to tell me more about Molly. With the relationship between her parents so poor, I suspected that Molly might have problems with intimacy and trust. That was true, Terry said. Molly had grown up a solitary child, and her interests—writing, science, and long-distance running—were solitary pursuits. In college and in medical school, she had begun to relate to others, but although she had a number of women friends, her social life was limited. Molly maintained that she would have plenty of time for relationships after she had gotten started in a career. She was still a virgin, and she was still a "loner." Most of her time was spent on her work.

Terry didn't find this lack of balance disturbing, perhaps because it mirrored her own. In fact, she was encouraging it by constantly insisting that Molly upgrade her performance in medical school. "I suppose you realize there's a lot more bothering Molly than her choice of career," I commented. The issue of Molly's damaged capacity for trust had to be addressed, too. Undoubtedly it was affecting not only her ability to get close to other people, but to commit to a career path as well.

My main point was to demonstrate to Terry how narrow

her exploration of the issues had been. Molly's relationship with both her parents had to be examined in greater depth. "I've heard a lot about her mother, but not too much about her father," I commented.

Terry's back stiffened. I could see the secret Terry begin to take charge. Why was she so anxious to keep the spotlight off Charles van der Cleer? Why did she feel such a need to protect him? And then I thought about Terry's father, the disabled factory worker. Terry had remembered loving him all the more in the face of her mother's mean-spiritedness. Perhaps Helene van der Cleer's selfishness had released the same protective feelings for Charles van der Cleer.

Terry did not address my comment about Molly's father. "You know, Wayne," she said, "I've been going over what you said a while ago, about my wanting to give Molly the support I never had from my own mother. That makes sense. It would account for my pushing her so strongly for medical school, and for neglecting other issues. I have a feeling I can be less dictatorial with Molly from now on. I certainly don't want to act like my mother."

The subject of motherly behavior opened the door to a sensitive issue I had wanted to discuss with Terry. Had she ever experienced a pregnancy of her own? If she had either had an abortion or relinquished a child to adoption, that might account for her need to re-create that child in her patient.

Terry's frank answer to my frank probing was "no." Then she had an afterthought. "If I'd ever been pregnant, Wayne, nothing on earth could have induced me to give up my child. You know how determined I am once I set my mind on something."

She went on to say that ten years ago, in her middle forties, she had been quite perturbed when she realized her biological clock was running out. "But I've long since adjusted to it, I'm sure of that," she commented. In fact, she said, her nurturing instincts had found other outlets, the mentoring of young therapists, for example, and her supportive attitude toward the members of our professional organization.

182

THE DREAM OF HAVING THE PERFECT CHILD

In spite of Terry's certainty, I thought that somewhere in her subconscious the dream of having her own child might remain. As she had said, when she fixed her mind on something, she was pretty determined. Was Molly the child Terry had set her heart on for some particular reason? For the present, I realized, I would have to be satisfied not with an answer to that question but with having made some progress. Terry had said she thought she could be less "dictatorial" with Molly, and over the next few weeks she reported success in that direction. She achieved it by assuming an "objective" stance, almost as if she was an observer in the therapy. It kept her from losing control and "coming down hard" on Molly, which was, apparently, something she still had an urge to do.

Detachment didn't sound ideal to me, but it was, after all, better than being judgmental. And apparently Terry's altered approach allowed Molly to "open up" and talk about her emotions. For some time, Molly said, she felt as if she was in a pressure cooker, but she thought she had no right to complain. After all, she had so many advantages: wealth, successful parents, and entrée into the worlds of medicine and literature. Her father and grandmother had simply assumed she would go to medical school. They did not have to talk about it. It was a given. "Their hearts would have been broken if I didn't go," Molly remarked. Busy as he was, her father had always found time for her. He had been the most loyal and loving person in her life. And his life was so lonely. How could she disappoint him?

Now that Molly was in medical school, her progress was a major topic of conversation between father and daughter. "He phones after every exam and asks how it went," Molly reported to Terry. "If I screw up, he tries not to sound disappointed, but I can tell he is." It didn't seem that Charles van der Cleer intended to lean on Molly—on the contrary, he always told her not to worry—but phone he did, and Molly experienced anxious feelings.

The result was that she found herself daydreaming with increasing frequency. She told Terry she imagined that she was anyplace but medical school, in a strange city or on a boat, for example. But most often she was running in the country. She had been a long-distance runner in college, but this type of running was different. She wasn't competing. She saw herself running through fields, up a mountainside, and from one road to another. All of the roads led to a small cabin. And once she got inside, she started to breathe more easily. The cabin was sparsely furnished but comfortable. There was no telephone. No one could reach her. Molly felt at peace.

When Terry told me about Molly's daydream, I wondered if Molly was running away from a career in medicine. "Is there a word processor in the cabin, by any chance?"

No, Terry said, there was nothing that could remind Molly of writing. "She didn't even mention a table, pens, or pencils. The place is practically empty. She fills it up herself. That's what she likes about it."

"Does she say what she does in the cabin?" I asked.

"Nothing."

It sounded to me as if the cabin might be a "holding place," a refuge where Molly could sort out her emotions and make some choices among many roads. The cabin could also replicate a safe maternal place which had been denied Molly by her mother's indifference.

Not unexpectedly, Molly's feelings about that maternal figure, Helene van der Cleer, were complicated and emerged over several sessions with Terry. At first, Molly's statements were bland. She admired her mother, she said, for her utter devotion to her talent. That was par for the course, I pointed out to Terry. Helene had set things up so that any attention she gave Molly was conditional upon the child's admiring her. Of course, admiration was what Molly must report feeling.

But after a while, Terry's objective attitude encouraged Molly to delve more deeply. She admitted to being very angry at her mother for abandoning her, so angry that she felt like tearing Helene to pieces. She had long despaired, she said, of receiving any real affection from her. The depth of her feelings frightened her, Molly remarked.

Then one day, she said the unthinkable. She told Terry she was not sure she liked her mother's writing very much. "It's boring," she admitted, "as if she's examining her navel all the time." Then she laughed. Although the laughter was somewhat hysterical, Terry realized it was the first time she had heard Molly laugh at all. She told Molly that she had a perfect right to come to her own conclusions about her mother's writing.

After this discussion, Terry reported that Molly was able to talk about both of her parents with less agitation. Neither, she felt, had the right to hassle her about career choice, although each was subtle enough—her father with his "collegial" inquiries into her progress and her mother with her habit of sending notices of writing workshops Molly had no time to attend. Because each of them had an ax to grind, she had told neither about her therapy, preferring to pay for it from a small trust fund her grandfather had left her.

Now Molly was glad she had kept the therapy to herself. She was coming to the conclusion that neither medicine nor writing were the right professions for her, at least not at present. She needed a "breather," she concluded. Once she verbalized this feeling, the daydreaming diminished.

Terry had every reason to feel pleased by Molly's progress. Her patient had succeeded in uncovering buried emotions, and although there was still a great deal more to be examined, Molly was moving toward making an independent decision. From my point of view, it was important that Terry had been able to keep her "dictatorial" parental feelings under control. I congratulated her.

"Thanks, Wayne," she said. "But believe me, those feelings are still there. It's all I can do to keep quiet. I think Molly's making a terrible mistake. I'm still sure she belongs in medicine."

"Terry," I broke in, "think about where you're coming from. You're 200 percent invested in medicine. How can you be objective?"

The mention of objectivity brought us to Terry's "new"

therapeutic approach. Although her detached attitude had borne fruit—and it was infinitely superior to beating Molly to death—it had inherent dangers. I told Terry that detachment can cause the death of treatment just as readily as overinvolvement, especially in a case like Molly's. Helene van der Cleer had been detached enough for one major figure in Molly's life. Ultimately, Terry's "objectivity" might, in Molly's mind, mirror Helene's indifference and cause her to transfer her anger at Helene to Terry.

Molly desperately needed an empathic, nonjudgmental approach in a therapist, as she had needed those qualities from her mother. I wouldn't be surprised, I said, if Molly started to test Terry in some way to see if she couldn't get an empathic response. And I told Terry I feared she might fail such a test because, despite her valiant efforts, her underlying attitude was just as parental as it was when she first walked into my office. And for all her studied detachment, she might still be communicating disapproval to Molly, by the way she looked, the words she used, or even the way she opened the door. Such are the subtleties of the relationship between therapist and patient. I urged Terry to get closer to what was blocking her empathy, the unresolved countertransference problem. Time was running short in finding the answer, I felt. Almost any unusual behavior on Molly's part could press Terry's buttons, with unfortunate results.

I was right to be concerned. Terry arrived for our next session desperately upset. A crisis had developed with Molly, she said, for which she blamed herself and perhaps me as well. "I should have been able to stop her, Wayne," she blurted.

"Stop her from what, Terry?"

Molly had embarked on an affair—with another woman. The woman, Susan, was a fellow medical student. The two had been friends for some time, and lately the friendship had grown stronger. One evening, after a long study session in Susan's room, they became lovers. Molly had been staying in the room ever since. "When I'm near Susan, I feel warm and safe," Molly had told Terry. "She knows what I'm thinking almost before I say it. And she makes me feel good about myself, too. Like I'm very special. Usually, I'm too shy to say 'boo' to anybody. But with her, it's like there are no barriers. It just seems right."

Molly was both thrilled by her new experience and made anxious by it. She had never been so close to another human being. She felt loved, yet she feared losing Susan at some time. And she didn't know how she honestly felt about "being gay."

Molly had really "opened up" to Terry, and the old judgmental Terry had reemerged with a vengeance. In her own words, she responded by "letting her have it." Terry told Molly that she had totally messed up this time. She wasn't really gay. She was rebelling against her family and against Terry, too.

If Terry had been dictatorial before, now she was a veritable juggernaut, rolling over Molly mercilessly. I had a vision of Molly crushed beneath her assault. I told Terry that rather than rebelling, Molly was probably trying to get the closeness she wanted from Terry—and her mother. "I suspect you're angry because she acted out her feelings with someone else," I suggested, not without a touch of annoyance.

Terry bit her lip. She didn't seem to be able to find the words to answer me. I wondered if I had come on too strong. I remembered that underneath she was fairly fragile.

"I'm sorry I was so blunt, Terry," I apologized. "Let's take it slowly. Why do you think you reacted the way you did? You're not a prejudiced person. You've worked with gay women in our society, and you've mentored some of them."

"I don't have a problem with homosexuality, Wayne. It's just that it's not right for Molly. I can't stand to see her messing up like this."

I suggested to Terry that we didn't yet know what the relationship with Susan meant to Molly. Once again, Terry was closing off an issue prematurely. I went on to say that although we don't always approve of our patient's decisions, we want them to be able to make decisions on their own. Molly was doing that now. And she was connecting in a vital way with another human being, which made her a damn sight better off than she was before.

Terry interrupted me. "I just can't buy it, Wayne," she said. "Molly's affair is having repercussions already. Something really terrible happened."

The "terrible" thing was that Molly and Susan had gone up to the Connecticut estate for the weekend. Molly said she wanted to show the place to Susan, and she knew that Helene would be away at a writers' seminar. The trip had a lot of implications, I thought, coming as it did right after the start of the affair. By making love on Helene's turf, Molly could be saying to her mother, "See, I found a woman to love me after all." She might be replacing Helene's activities by having an affair in the hideaway where her mother had had so many lovers of her own. She might have wanted to set Terry off. Or, quite possibly, all three.

But Terry wasn't thinking about any of this. What disturbed her was the fact that Molly and Susan had been seen by a neighbor, an old friend of the van der Cleers. The young women were having dinner at a local restaurant, and the neighbor was seated nearby. Molly thought that the neighbor may have "suspected something" because she and Susan had been looking at each other affectionately and, every so often, they linked hands across the table. The neighbor had a "funny expression" on her face, Molly imagined. She had told Terry the story because it was her first experience of what it might be like to be out in public with a lover of the same sex.

For Terry, this incident was the last straw. She had reacted vehemently, accusing Molly of having a pathological need to let the whole town know about her relationship. Molly had left the session in tears and Terry was not certain she would be back.

I told Terry that if Molly did not show up for her next appointment, she had to call her. If Molly did not want to see her anymore, Terry must recommend another therapist. But most important, I advised Terry to go back into therapy herself. She had to learn why she needed to force Molly to be not only a doctor but a heterosexual doctor.

When Terry left my office that day, she was the picture of dejection. She didn't like to fail, she said, and to her, going back into therapy represented a form of failure. She always moved on in life, and now she would be moving backwards.

I tried to encourage Terry by reminding her that it was sometimes necessary to go backwards in order to go forward, but truth to tell, I felt dejected myself. I didn't like to fail either, and this supervision wasn't bearing any fruit. In fact, Molly was now in a more precarious position than she had been when Terry began seeing me. As for Terry, she was still deeply mired in a countertransference problem.

I went over my last session with Terry, attempting to put the pieces together one more time. I wanted to get at the secret Terry. Was she the embattled adolescent, trying to shelter her father from her mother's assaultive tongue? Or the vulnerable nurse coming to medical school in New York? Or the successful physician, struggling to come to terms with her childlessness in middle age?

Images began to stir in my mind, and I struggled fiercely to bring them to consciousness. A number of times in therapeutic sessions, I had found that meaningful interpretations first emerged as visual images. Once, for example, something I pictured called to mind the title of a book that illuminated a patient's problem. This visualization process hasn't received much attention in the literature, and there's much to be learned about it. I only know that it works for me, and it may for other therapists as well.

So now I encouraged it by closing my eyes and leaning back in my chair. I saw the photograph of Charles van der Cleer sitting alone on the dais. Suddenly, he wasn't alone. There was a figure in the chair next to him. It was Terry and she had her arm on his in a reassuring fashion.

Charles van der Cleer, I realized, was the key figure in what was going on. I had been too quick to move away from the subject of Charles when Terry became upset by it. If he represented her father in some way, perhaps her relationship with her father was more problematic than I had realized. Or, Charles could be associated in Terry's mind with another love object, perhaps her dead therapist. Whatever he represented, it was time to unmask the "Charles connection."

At our next session, I was pleased to learn that Molly had kept her appointment with Terry. And that Terry had arranged an appointment for herself with a therapist, someone we both knew from our professional society.

So far so good, I thought. "Terry," I said, "I've been reviewing Molly's affair with Susan. You said that Molly wasn't sure how she felt about 'being gay.' Do you know if she thinks her family might disapprove?"

"Well, it's not likely that her mother would. She scarcely gives a thought to Molly anyway."

"What about her father?" I asked.

Terry became agitated. "That's just it, Wayne," she said. "Molly is quite certain her father wouldn't mind. He's always taken a very open-minded attitude in their discussions about sex, which were theoretical, of course. What she doesn't realize is that when it comes right down to it, he'll be very upset. Charles van der Cleer is actually very close-minded when it comes to homosexuality."

How did she know, I asked? There was a pause, while I let Terry think about what she had revealed. A curtain of stillness descended in the room and I was aware of only two things: Terry's quiet breathing and my own. Finally, she broke the silence. Charles van der Cleer, she said, had been her lover in medical school.

Her confession made my head spin. How could an ethical therapist, a straightforward person like Terry, undertake to treat her former lover's child?

Terry reacted to my question with extreme emotion, experiencing relief, I suspected, as well as guilt and shame. She started to hyperventilate, as she had during our previous discussion of Charles. Once again, she fled to the window, leaned on the air conditioner, and let the cool air run over her flushed face.

I walked up behind her and put my hand on her shoulder. "I know this is rough," I said. Terry nodded wordlessly and I guided her back to her chair.

"It was wrong of me, I know," she murmured, "but I honestly believed I was completely over Charles. I hadn't thought of him in years. So when our mutual friend, Herb, told me about Molly's problem, I thought I could be helpful. After all, I knew what the family was like."

Terry's veneer of strength crumbled, and she broke into tears. She seemed to have grown smaller in seconds, and younger. Here before my eyes was the secret Terry. I moved my chair closer to hers, resettled myself, and insisted gently that she tell me the whole story. Now it was really no-bullshit time.

The story began with Terry's first months in New York, when she was determined to succeed in medical school, yet frightened. Everything—the amount of work required, the big city itself—seemed overwhelming. Charles van der Cleer, a second-year student, befriended her. He gave her the "scoop" on various professors. He showed her how to get around on the subway. He took her to art galleries and to the theater. He opened a window on a new world.

Charles was more than an urbane New Yorker, more than the well-mannered scion of a socially prominent family. He was a naturally kind and giving man. When she was with him, Terry felt totally secure. She was able to tell him about her family and her struggles. He seemed to understand everything. He admired her for her frankness and her spirit of independence. Charles himself was under the thumb of his family, he confided to Terry. Rather like the Prince of Wales, he was obliged to "go into the family business" and live up to expectations. When Terry asked why, he simply replied that was the way it was.

Their friendship blossomed into romance and then into a very passionate affair. Terry was in love forever, she thought.

Charles said he felt the same way and they made plans to marry. But they had not anticipated the reaction of the van der Cleers. Even though Charles's parents didn't know Terry well, they decided she was "unsuitable." Her background was inferior, her forthright style was grating, and she was a few years older than Charles.

The van der Cleers did everything they could to undermine the "engagement" without actually tossing Terry out the door. She felt increasingly uncomfortable. Charles felt increasingly anxious, but he was too passive a character to oppose his family for long. The strain began to tell in his schoolwork and his love life. The spontaneity went out of his relationship with Terry. "When we were together, we really weren't together anymore," she recalled. "There was a great big book standing between us—the Social Register."

Terry realized she had to let Charles go, that he had already gone, in fact. But after they parted, she was "totally broken up." She filled the void with increased dedication to her studies and, later in her career, when Charles still seemed to be unreplaceable, with patients, writing, and work in the professional association. A few years after he and Terry broke up, Charles married Helene. In every superficial way—looks, background, social graces—Helene was "suitable." Yet psychologically, she was "unsuitable," incapable of loving anyone. The marriage turned out to be a disaster. The couple split apart in anger, each feeling victimized, but there was another victim, the child, Molly.

Terry had learned about all this from Herb, the old family friend. Charles's situation produced a flood of conflicting emotions: sorrow, satisfaction—she had, after all, been dumped —and guilt. By letting Charles go, she had unwittingly exposed him to greater unhappiness than she would have by marrying him. Perhaps she should have fought harder. Clearly, he needed her to protect him.

These feelings lingered until Terry was in her middle thirties and they occasioned her decision to go into therapy. It was hard work, and it wasn't complete at the time her therapist died. Still, Terry was certain that her ties to Charles were broken. All of the emotions she associated with him were gone. As far as she was concerned, their affair was something that had happened in the past, and Molly was just another referral.

But when she started treating Molly, she found herself behaving oddly, talking "as if the words were coming out of someone else's mouth." It didn't occur to her that she might be speaking Charles's words. He would have wanted Molly to stay in medical school. Terry would see to it that she did. He disliked homosexuality. She would keep Molly straight.

All these years, Terry had subconsciously nurtured a child, the child that might have been hers with Charles. This child would have bound Charles to her irrevocably. By turning Molly into the perfect child for Charles, she could reunite herself with him. He would realize what a mistake he had made in not marrying her all those long years ago.

There were other aspects to Terry's subconscious fantasy. By creating the perfect child, Terry could repair her own childlessness and her own imperfections. She would become a new Terry, a version of herself the van der Cleers couldn't have rejected. Thus, the trauma and pain of the past would be redressed.

As Terry and I talked about all this, she became calmer. Part of what I was saying, of course, had been in her mind all the time, but under the heavy wraps of repression. "You know, Wayne," she remarked, "I wonder if I didn't come to you because I wanted you to find out the truth and stop me. Maybe I selected a no-bullshit supervisor because underneath I knew I was bullshitting myself."

The trouble was that Terry had been bullshitting Molly, too. The issue of what to do about Molly's therapy was now uppermost in both our minds. Terry wanted to continue to treat Molly, and I thought it was important that she continue, too. Molly had been emotionally abandoned by Helene. If Terry, whom she had trusted, also walked out on her, the impact could be severe. Molly needed an ongoing relationship, and Terry could provide that.

Yet having Terry go on with Molly was risky. Substantial therapy would be required for Terry to work through her feelings about Charles. In the meantime, there was a danger that her dream of the perfect child would continue to have an impact on Molly. We both agreed, however, that it was worth taking the risk, as long as Terry remained under close supervision. Being aware of the reason for the countertransference was a major step forward. In a fairly short time, I thought, Terry could emerge as the caring figure Molly needed. We decided to have Terry continue the treatment.

At her next session with Molly, Terry apologized for her past behavior, without revealing her connection to Charles van der Cleer. Therapists don't often apologize, but apologizing—if it doesn't become a habit with a particular patient—can clear the air and increase a patient's confidence. That's what happened in Molly's case, and fortunately things went well with the treatment from then on. Terry became increasingly empathic and Molly increasingly able to make her own decisions.

By the time I stopped supervising Terry, Molly was enrolled in law school, and she was still living with Susan. As for Charles van der Cleer, I suppose he adapted himself to the situation, because Terry reported that he and Molly were still close and that Susan was a frequent visitor to the Connecticut estate when Helene was away, as she never accepted the situation.

So parents can learn to be more flexible, and so can therapists. And as for the dream of the perfect child, it is only a dream. It is far more rewarding to come to terms with the reality of our children.

CHAPTER 9

The Dream of Sadism

T he term "sadism" was coined only a century ago, but it describes a perversion as old as human nature itself: getting a kick out of hurting others. It need not involve inflicting actual physical pain. There is a subtle sadism in which the sadist uses mere words to hurt others emotionally.

If a therapist suffers from this problem, it's easy for him or her to beat up on patients under the worthy banner of getting them to "face the truth" about themselves. After all, that's the goal of therapy, isn't it? The profession would seem to allow the therapist to release his or her own destructive anger in the guise of being helpful. And patients often think they are in treatment when in reality they are in an emotional trap. Unfortunately, a sadistic therapist can be difficult to spot, as the story of Edie shows.

When I first met Edie in the summer of 1986, I had no reason to think she was anything but what she seemed to be, an effervescent and caring person. We were in the middle of a heat wave and my air conditioner was on the blink. But the oppressive heat that dampened her face hardly dampened her spirits, which any observer would have described as "bubbly." With her light brown hair piled up on her head, her neat figure encased in a shirtwaist dress, and her shapely legs crossed as she leaned forward to talk to me, she looked and sounded like a young Debbie Reynolds. Many of her comments concluded with a lilting inflection of enthusiasm. She and I were in such an important field, she observed, so much opportunity to make a difference in people's lives—but of course, she laughed self-deprecatingly, with my years of experience, I must know all that.

Edie herself had been a licensed psychologist for seven years and was in her middle thirties. She worked at a treatment center in the suburbs that was connected to a state mental hospital. Recently, the center had gotten a contract to do research in geriatric psychotherapy, so it would be handling many more older patients.

The notion of doing psychotherapy with older people is fairly new. Traditionally, senior citizens have gotten short shrift from therapists, the belief being that they are too set in their ways for therapy to be effective. But recent research has shown that emotional development doesn't cease after young adulthood, as was previously thought. Indeed, the life experiences of older people, the losses they endure, may even make them more amenable to change than other age groups.

I'm a strong advocate of psychodynamically oriented therapy with older patients, and Edie had heard me speak on the subject. It was because of this talk that she had contacted me. Since she would be seeing more older patients, she said, she wanted my help in developing her expertise. She was already treating one older patient, a seventy-three-year-old man who was depressed following his wife's death in a car crash. Edie planned to discuss this case with me, and whatever new ones came up. She was already "one up" on the subject of the elderly, she said, since she had been raised by her grandparents.

"My parents died in a boating accident when I was five, and my paternal grandparents became responsible for me," she recounted, the lilt going out of her voice temporarily. "They were the only relatives I had left."

"It must have been rough on all of you," I remarked.

"Rough, yes, that's the right word," Edie replied, dabbing

her eyes with a tissue, whether to remove perspiration or tears I couldn't tell.

Edie went on to say she had been in therapy herself. The treatment, she thought, had enabled her to work through her feelings about losing her parents. "And things have really come out okay for me," she said. "I have a wonderful family now."

She took out her wallet and showed me a photograph of her husband, Tom, and their one-year-old daughter. Although I didn't ask, Edie described the marriage as a happy one. Tom, a cardiologist, was "a wonderful person," and their daughter "a joy." The only fly in the ointment was Tom's mother, a whiny and demanding woman who, Edie said, had driven Tom's father into the arms of another woman. "Even to this day, she doesn't realize she made him leave her," Edie commented, in an unusually strident tone.

She fixed her cool gray eyes on me, giving me my first experience of her memorable stare. "Stare" is the wrong word, actually. It was more like being fixed under a pin and dissected. But just as I was becoming uneasy, the stare disappeared, the cold eyes warmed up, and the button nose crinkled. Had the stare really happened? It didn't seem possible. Now the blithe spirit who had fairly danced into my office was back.

"Well, I guess Mom's not my problem, is she?" Edie said brightly. "As long as she stays in Chicago and only visits once a year. Though that's due to happen soon. Oh, well, I suppose I'll survive."

Because of the heat, we agreed to cut the session short, but I told Edie I would be happy to take her on as a supervisee. "You won't be sorry, Wayne." She smiled as she shook my hand and floated toward the door.

And for the next few weeks, I certainly wasn't sorry. It was a joy to watch Edie's handling of her seventy-three-year-old patient. The patient was driving when his wife was killed in the crash, but he wasn't responsible for the accident. A drunken teenager had hit the car head on. Nevertheless, he suffered strong feelings of guilt, which are natural after such an event. The survivor feels depressed at the loss and guilt at being alive. But when guilt persists, as it had in the case of Edie's patient, it points to problems in the broken relationship. Getting to the heart of these problems can be quite delicate, but Edie's instincts were sound and sure. She didn't make the beginner's mistake of trying to move too quickly. Instead, she listened and supported her patient until he was ready to talk about his long-standing rage toward his wife, and finally, of his relief at her death. It was these feelings, rather than grief, that fueled his guilt and depression.

"Such an unhappy situation," Edie commented to me, "but I finally got the truth out of him."

"How did you do that?" I inquired.

"Oh, I just kept at him, gently of course. I knew from what he said over the past few weeks that he must have hated her, but he had to be the one to acknowledge that. And, finally, he did," she summed up, with satisfaction.

It sounded like a reasonable approach, I thought. An insight is only valuable when the patient comes to it himself. Edie had enabled her patient to develop insight by using just the right combination of empathy, skill, and patience. That combination is very rare in younger therapists working with older patients, simply because they haven't had the life experiences that allow them to understand what the elderly are going through.

Edie, however, had had an early experience with something that usually affects older people—grief. Her grief appeared to have been resolved, however, which meant, I thought, that her grandparents must have handled it well. Young children don't usually resolve their grief unless they are encouraged to grieve by their caretakers or a therapist. In Edie's case, her early losses seemed to have given her an expanded capacity for empathy, and this worked to the advantage of her patients.

The elderly gentleman, for example, was recovering rapidly from depression, and he and Edie were making plans to terminate treatment. He was going to volunteer his time, he said, at Mothers Against Drunk Driving. This was an activity that Edie had suggested would give meaning to his wife's death and allow him to repair their relationship by reaching out to others. It sounded like a positive step, indeed.

"What a sad time he's had," Edie commented. And once again, I was struck by her high quotient of compassion for others. At least, that's what I thought it was.

A short time later, I believed I saw more of that compassion when Edie started treating her second older patient. This patient's story was also a tragic one. Vera Duna, sixty-five, had lost her only son, Michael, thirty-five, to an overdose of drugs six months previously. Vera was depressed, but her other child, Therese, Michael's twin, was even more devastated. And as the months went on, Therese's grief increased instead of lessening. Finally, she was so depressed, she was unable to function at all. Vera contacted the treatment center, and the director, a psychiatrist, admitted Therese to the state hospital. The psychiatrist tried several types of antidepressants with Therese, but she failed to respond adequately to any of them. Finally, electric shock treatment was planned.

It was at this juncture that Edie first learned about the Dumas. The psychiatrist was discussing the case at a staff conference at the treatment center and remarked that, in his view, Vera Duna required therapy. Not only had she suffered a great loss, she now had to deal with a very sick daughter. Concerned that she might break down, he suggested that she seek treatment at the center, and Vera agreed.

Edie immediately asked that Vera be assigned to her. She felt that treating the depressed widower had given her a particularly sensitivity toward bereaved older people. Besides, Vera's case touched her heart. To have a son die and a daughter become so ill—Edie could just imagine how decimated she herself would be by such events. And from what the psychiatrist had said, Vera was pretty much alone in the world.

Edie began to work with Vera, and at the very first session she projected enormous empathy. It must be a terrible burden, she said, to have to care for a sick daughter when one needed to be cared for oneself. Vera began to weep copiously. No one had understood that before. According to Edie, a strong bond was rapidly established between her and Vera. Vera made an easy transference to Edie, seeing her, Edie thought, as a competent and sustaining daughter. I agreed with that assessment. It's common for an older person to establish a "filial transference," in which the therapist becomes an idealized child, the type of child, perhaps, the patient would have liked to have. In many cases, the therapist becomes more than a transference figure and an actual object in the patient's life, since the patient may not have many people left to depend on.

Although Vera was the type of person who usually kept her troubles to herself, Edie's support enabled her to talk about her concerns. In the forefront of her mind was Therese's condition. No one, including Therese's psychiatrist, understood how frightened Vera was by her daughter's illness. The idea of this electric shock treatment terrified her. What if something went wrong?

Edie reassured Vera. "The treatment is perfectly safe," she said. "Patients are sedated beforehand and, during the procedure, they're given anesthetics. There's no pain, and the results are usually quite good."

Edie told me that Vera still looked uncertain, so she explained further. "You're probably thinking of the old days when patients were strapped down and restrained by nurses as the electric current was administered. The pain of that first jolt was searing. The patients' eyes would roll back in their heads, and their mouths jerked open. Sometimes, a person could flail around wildly, sometimes breaking bones or causing some other damage. But that kind of thing doesn't happen anymore. And the results are quite good—that is, most of the time."

Vera seemed disturbed by this description and said she didn't want to talk about it anymore. Edie was taken aback. "It's amazing the way some patients can just shut off a topic when they don't want to think about it," she remarked.

"Well," I replied, "you might have told Vera much more than she wanted to know. In fact, it sounds as if listening to you gave her the shock treatment."

"I just thought she deserved to know the facts, Wayne," Edie replied mildly enough, but once again fixing me with her stare. I looked away uncomfortably.

Still I managed to say that hitting Vera over the head didn't seem necessary, particularly when the woman had been through so much. To myself, I wondered why Edie thought pounding out all that information was necessary. I would watch to see whether this type of overkill happened again.

In the meantime, I was anxious to hear her patient's life story, and Edie obligingly told it to me. Vera Duna was born in Hungary a few years after the end of World War I. The war left her large family even more impoverished than it was before, and as the 1920s progressed, things got worse. Vera remembered her mother and neighbor women rummaging through garbage cans in the rich neighborhoods of Budapest, looking for food. Little Vera stood close to her mother, so that she could hide whatever morsels her mother slipped to her in her clothing. She learned early that life was tough, and that there wasn't always enough of things—food, clothes, or love—to share with others.

During World War II, the family suffered more deprivation. One brother, a member of the underground, was killed. Vera was pressed into working in a factory that shipped arms to Germany. After the war and the Communist takeover of Hungary, Vera married Gyorgi Duna, a high school history teacher. Gyorgi's position was fairly well paid and with Vera's job in a department store, the couple acquired enough money to purchase a cottage in the suburbs. They furnished it bit by bit, and Vera loved every object in it. After the twins were born, she left her job and stayed home with them.

Gyorgi was an intellectual who felt stifled by communism, but he was resigned to spending his life in what he called its "gray prison." Vera was not quite as dissatisfied, and unlike Gyorgi, she had many brothers and sisters who bound her to the country of her birth. Then in October 1956, as revolution broke out in Budapest, Gyorgi got the chance he never thought he would have—to flee the country. The decision had to be made quickly, before Russian tanks succeeded in quelling the revolt. There was scarcely time for Vera to debate the matter with him. "It's best for the children," he said one night, settling the argument.

The next morning, Gyorgi put a few of the twins' clothes and toys in a shopping bag. "If anyone asks," he told Vera, "we're going to visit your sister." Vera slipped two gold rings that had belonged to her grandmother on her fingers. Then the family put on their coats and walked out of their house, not even bothering to lock the door. With the parents holding the children's hands, they walked straight for the border and eventually crossed into Austria. The twins were five years old at the time.

The following year, the Dunas came to the United States. Here everything was different, exciting but frightening. There were no jobs for teachers who knew little English and even less about American history. Vera and Gyorgi had to start all over again. They worked at whatever jobs they could find, trying to arrange their schedules so that one of them was always home with the twins. If that was impossible, they left them with a neighbor who cared for a number of children in her apartment.

Later, when the Dunas started their own importing business, they had to depend on that neighbor even more. The business took almost all of their time, and Vera quickly became the dominant figure in it. She seemed to have the hard-nosed business sense to hassle with exporters and customers, while Gyorgi tended to be dreamy and inappropriately optimistic. He always thought things would work out for the best. He could never see the bad in people, Vera told Edie, even if they robbed him blind. His character was "softer" than hers.

Gyorgi was the one the children went to for comfort and support, while Vera took on the major burdens of the business. Tough as she appeared to be, Vera missed her relatives in Hungary desperately. "But I could never let on," she confided to Edie. "I had to be the iron one."

From their first days in the United States, Vera said, Michael was a problem. In school, he got into fights with other children. He told lies and he stole things. His classmates avoided him. His only friend was his sister, Therese, whom Vera termed "a timid soul."

Vera would lose her temper with Michael and even strike him, but Gyorgi never did those things. He was a saint. Matters grew even worse when Michael became a teenager and started using drugs. At first, Vera didn't know about the habit. Gyorgi kept it from her. He slipped Michael money, pretending to himself that Michael was using it for other things. But he knew. And over time, as Michael's behavior became more bizarre, Vera developed suspicions of her own. Finally, when the petty cash slips failed to balance for the hundredth time, she demanded that Gyorgi tell her the truth. Even after she knew the truth, Vera didn't interfere with Gyorgi's slipping Michael money. She went along with Gyorgi's fantasy that Michael was merely unhappy and needed the drugs to make him "feel a bit better." As to when Michael would find a job, that too would come "in time."

But time ran out for Gyorgi first. He had died of cancer two years ago, and after his death Vera stopped giving cash to Michael, who was living "heaven knows where." But he got money, she knew, by stealing from others and even from her. Sometimes, after Michael's visits, she would find her purse empty. Then there would be objects missing from the house. These objects had replaced the ones she left in the cottage in Hungary and they were precious to her, but Michael seemed to have no idea of that.

Finally, after the house was broken into a few times by thieves that Vera suspected were friends of Michael's, she asked him not to visit anymore. Therese, who lived with Vera, was quite upset. She begged her mother to change her mind, but Vera stood firm. Then one night, Vera and Therese came home to find that the two gold rings Vera had worn when she left Hungary were missing. This was the last straw. Vera had the locks changed, and she got a court order forbidding Michael from coming near the house.

The night the order went into effect, Vera heard Therese talking on the telephone in a low voice. A while later, Therese went out. Vera looked through her daughter's drawers, where she usually kept her money, and found that most of Therese's cash was missing. She suspected that Therese had gone to give the money to Michael. The next morning, Michael was found dead of a drug overdose in an alley in New York City.

"Michael's death would probably have been devastating enough, but Vera had had so many other losses in her life," I commented.

"That's just it, Wayne," Edie beamed at me. "I know that helping her deal with loss is the major issue here. But Vera's got to feel a lot of anger, too. She'll need plenty of support until she's ready to talk about it."

Unlike the discussion about electric shock treatment, Edie seemed to be on target here. Her supportive stance would help Vera work through her grief and deal with emotions she might not yet be aware of. I suspected, however, that Vera, who struck me as a realist, must be in touch with some of the anger she harbored toward her son.

Edie told me it wasn't long before Vera was able to discuss her feelings. Edie was, in her view, "such a nice young lady," and besides, no one had ever before been interested in her emotions. When she was a child, she told Edie, there was "no time for such a thing as feelings." Everyone in Vera's family had to concentrate on simply staying alive. That was true all the way through World War II. Even when her brother was killed, the family couldn't mourn publicly for fear of revealing his connection to the underground.

When she married Gyorgi, Vera thought she was at last financially and emotionally secure. But then he insisted on going to America in search of "an ideal," forcing her to leave her brothers and sisters. No sooner had she absorbed that loss than she had to adjust to life in a new country.

It quickly became apparent that she couldn't lean on Gyorgi. Rather, it would be the other way around. She girded herself up to be "the boss." Her head was always full of financial problems, it seemed, and Michael made everything worse, tugging at her skirts, whining after her not to leave him, when she was forced to go to work so that there would be "food on the table." "Even when I was three years old, I knew what that meant—putting food on the table," she exclaimed to Edie. But Michael never understood. He seemed to want all of her.

And then the trouble she had with him, getting called to school by the teachers, having to miss time at work. Here, again, Gyorgi was no help at all. He even encouraged Michael to be what Vera called "a baby." They had many arguments about it, especially after Michael got into drugs. But Gyorgi never made Michael "act like a man."

Vera acknowledged her anger toward Michael. He had always been a nuisance, she said, and he had killed his father by breaking his heart. After Gyorgi's death, she stopped giving Michael money so he would come to his senses. But that didn't solve the problem. In fact, Michael made more trouble as he took to stealing. This was the final shame. "Do you know what we did to thieves when I was a child in Hungary?" Vera asked Edie. "People would tear them limb from limb. That's how we protected what we had."

The night that Vera came home and found her grandmother's rings missing, a gun went off in her head. She remembered the way her grandmother had wanted to sell those rings for food in the 1920s, but her grandfather had forbidden her. He called the rings family heirlooms. Vera was horrified that Michael had taken the rings and given them to his "dirty friends" to sell for drugs. There was no recourse, as she saw it, but to get the court order. With his main source of goods cut off, Michael would have to learn to stand on his own two feet. She never expected him to overdose instead. The news of his death devastated her. It seemed to be the final blow in a life filled with loss and no real luck or happiness.

Then, even more trouble developed. Vera had to bear the brunt of Therese's depression, hospitalizing her and worrying about her treatment. But now, thank goodness, the electric shock treatment seemed to be working. Therese was coming out of her depression, as was Vera, with Edie's help and a course of antidepressant medication.

"Vera's certainly sharing a lot with you," I commented to Edie. "And that can't be easy, after being so tight-lipped all her life. She must really trust you."

Edie looked pleased. She pressed her fingers together and glanced up at the ceiling, as if speculating about the way things would go now.

"We're only at the beginning, I think," she said. "I've just started to tap into her anger. She was furious at Michael, but I'm not sure she realizes how mad she is at Gyorgi, and particularly at Therese for giving Michael money the night before he died."

"Not as angry as Therese is at herself," I reflected. "She probably blames herself for her brother's death. That might be why she's been in such a severe depression." I went on to advise Edie not to push the idea of anger too much with Vera. She had already admitted to quite a bit of it, and squeezing out every last drop of anger doesn't do wonders for a patient's self-esteem. It's particularly counterproductive in the treatment of depression where the patient's self-esteem is already quite low. The object here is to raise self-image, not lower it further.

"You're probably right, Wayne," Edie said a bit dubiously in response to my comments. "I'll try not to upset the apple cart with Vera. Things are going well with her."

Things were going well for Edie, too, she told me. "My mother-in-law came for her annual visit last week," she reported, "and it went okay. She can be such a pain. But this time, I finally got her to see how she pushes people away by being so demanding."

"How exactly did you manage that?" I asked, my interest piqued by the thought of achieving such speedy insight.

Edie was more than happy to tell me her secret. "First of all, it's a matter of caring," she bubbled. "Most people don't bother enough about others to give them the facts. Second, it's finding the right opportunity to really talk to the person."

In the case of Edie's mother-in-law, that opportunity had arisen when Tom, Edie's husband, took their daughter to the playground. Edie and her mother-in-law stayed home and watched a Bette Davis movie on cable television. In this particular film, Davis played a very devious and demanding character, turning people against her left and right. Edie remarked to her mother-in-law that she sometimes acted just like Bette Davis. Oh, not by doing everything she did in the movies, but just some of them, like putting people down, for example. From there, it was easy to get to the reason for some other "problems," such as why Mom's husband had left her. Edie felt she had really cleared the air.

I wasn't quite as happy with this report as Edie was. "It sounds as if you went for the jugular," I remarked. "It can't be easy for her to think of herself as a bitch who pushes people away."

Edie said nothing, but I could tell she was annoyed. Her gray eyes flickered, but she didn't bother to turn on the stare. Instead, she busied herself with getting her things together.

"I shouldn't have burdened you with my story, Wayne," she commented in a clipped tone, not unlike Bette Davis herself. "After all, my mother-in-law isn't part of your supervisory responsibilities." Then she headed for the door.

I had been tough on her, I thought, as I heard the door slam, maybe even a little sadistic. But was it really sadism, or was I subconsciously standing up for her mother-in-law in a way that Mom was unable to do herself? "Gentle" Edie had unsheathed some pretty sharp claws. There was something worrisome about the way she went on the attack with her mother-in-law and something equally worrisome about her need to ferret out Vera's "anger."

I speculated that both "somethings" probably came down to one countertransference problem that was directed toward older people. That problem, whatever it was, might be the real reason Edie had sought my supervision. I realized that I had to watch the treatment of Vera very carefully to protect that elderly lady from getting an overdose of "insight."

At our next session, Edie had still more to tell me about Vera's anger.

"I thought we'd agreed to go easy on anger," I reminded her. "I know," Edie replied, "but she insisted on discussing this."

Michael wasn't the only child Vera was angry at, Edie told me. For many years, it seemed, Vera had harbored resentment against Therese as well. Even as a child, Therese was shy and withdrawn. Now, at thirty-five, she had few friends, no boyfriends, and lived at home. She wasn't much of a companion, and she would never be able to take care of Vera when Vera became infirm. Instead, she was just another burden. One only had to look at Therese's reaction to Michael's death to see that.

"She called Therese an emotional cripple, just like her brother," Edie sputtered. "That really ticked me off. After all, there's poor Therese, sitting in the hospital barely able to tie her shoelaces. And all Vera thinks about is herself. What a selfish bitch she is."

This was a different Edie, full of anger at her patient. She seemed to have lost sight of the fact that she had created rapport with Vera by empathizing with her burdens. Now all that empathy seemed to have disappeared. Yet the success of the treatment depended on Edie's empathy. I had to get her back on track.

"Vera's always managed by being self-reliant," I commented. "But at this stage in her life, she wants someone to lean on. She thought you'd be there for her no matter what feelings she revealed. But you're so angry, you're not keeping your end of the bargain. She's got to be tuning into that."

Edie looked concerned. "I want to be there for Vera, I really do," she sighed. "But it's hard when I realize what a terrible mother she's been, neglecting her children under the guise of having to put food on the table. Treating them as if they were burdens. I think she ought to face up to all that."

I told Edie that "facing up" to everything wasn't always the best idea. Besides, I wasn't sure that things were as black and white with the Dunas as she was making them. After all, Vera was the one who had kept the family together, while Gyorgi "wimped out." And even if Vera had done some things wrong, coercing a patient into self-knowledge isn't treatment, it's mental rape.

I saw that Edie was quite resistant to what I was saying. Her need to make people see the truth about themselves was apparently so strong it could be destructive. She was a therapeutic Grand Inquisitor, using her insight as an instrument of torture. She had made her mother-in-law "confess" to heaven knows what. And now I wondered about the elderly gentleman she had treated before Vera. Had he really hated his wife? Or had he finally succumbed to Edie's relentless stare? I suspected the latter. When I had asked Edie a few weeks ago if she knew how he was doing, she had been quite vague, which gave me some pause.

The insights I was developing about Edie had to make me curious about the issues that had come up in her own therapy. Since therapy is a very private matter, and not really part of the supervisory process, I approached the subject with care. I told Edie she seemed very angry at Vera and her mother-in-law. I wasn't trying to pry, but I wondered if she had talked about anger in her treatment. I wondered, too, about her grandparents. What had they been like?

"I scarcely knew them," Edie replied.

"But I thought you said they raised you," I remarked, surprised.

"I said they were responsible for me. But that doesn't mean I had too much to do with them."

Edie's grandmother had been an invalid, she told me, who "just couldn't hack" taking care of a small child. Her grandfather had been busy taking care of his wife. So until Edie was old enough to go away to boarding schools, the couple hired a series of live-in girls to "look after" her.

"It was a large country house, and I really didn't see my grandparents too much," Edie recalled. "I hardly ever remember having dinner with them. When summer vacations came, they shipped me right off to camp. What bugged me the most is that they showed up at all my graduations, Grandmom in her wheelchair, looking so proud. They weren't even aware of how they had neglected me."

Edie had brought up her anger in her therapy. Her grandparents were still alive at the time, and the therapist had suggested that she confront them with "the truth" of her feelings. Edie had done so, but all she accomplished was to drain off her own anger temporarily and leave her grandparents bewildered at her ingratitude. Well, there are all kinds of therapists out there, I thought.

Still, Edie believed the confrontation with her grandparents had been "helpful." "At least, getting it off my chest made me feel better," she said.

"Well, getting off on your own anger is one thing," I observed, "but beating your patients to death with it is quite another."

I told Edie that she had to concentrate not on anger but on Vera's unmet dependency needs. Otherwise, she would not get better. Vera needed someone to lean on, and since Therese was not equipped to be that someone, Edie had to be the dependable element in Vera's life. If Vera herself felt cared for, she might be able to be more caring toward her daughter. She might even be able to develop new relationships at some point.

Edie agreed to follow my prescription, although I sensed it would be difficult for her. But even as we talked, an event was taking place that would make it impossible for her to keep her promise. That very afternoon, Vera went to the mental hospital to visit Therese. When she arrived, she found Therese looking better, sitting by the window reading a book.

Therese was usually quite tentative with her mother, intimidated by her in fact. But now, as she recovered from the electric shock treatment, she was having therapeutic sessions with the psychiatrist who had hospitalized her and she had begun to realize that she was quite dissatisfied with her relationship with Vera. She was angry at the way Vera had neglected her and made her feel of little consequence. What saddened Therese was that Vera didn't seem to think of her as a person but as an unwanted appendage. Had she ever said anything to her at all beyond "Therese, do this" or "Therese, do that"? And had Therese ever said more than "Yes, Mama" or "No, Mama"? For the first time, Therese didn't think this was right.

The therapy sessions had given her a different outlook. They made Therese feel anxious, yet excited, as if she was learning something that had to be learned, something that might make her life more free. Now, as Vera came into the room, Therese eyed her uneasily. Today, she wanted to say more than "Yes, Mama."

"You are looking well," Vera stated emphatically, as if her words could make it so.

"I'm feeling better, Mama," Therese replied in a low voice.

"When will you come home?" Vera inquired.

Therese said that the doctor wasn't quite sure. But there was something important she wanted to discuss. When she did come home, she wanted things to be different. She wanted Vera to pay more attention to her, to value her. She wanted them to have conversations and go places together, like two grown-up women. "I want you to care about me, Mama," she implored.

Vera could make neither head nor tail of Therese's requests. She saw them as just another set of demands, demands she was ill-equipped to handle. In her confusion, she shrugged her shoulders, simply to indicate she didn't know what was going on, but Therese viewed the shrug as a turndown.

"I'm nothing to you, Mama," she cried. "I never was."

"Nothing to me?" Vera responded. "I carried you past the Russian tanks in my arms. Where would you be without me? You're just a big baby. And I don't need a grown-up baby, with all my problems."

Therese was angry enough to fight back. She said that not only had Vera made her sick, she had made Michael sick, too. She was the person responsible for Michael's addiction. "You called him a bum, Mama," Therese whimpered. "You called him a bum, when he was suffering so much. Where was your heart?" Therese began to cry.

"No matter what I called him, I didn't open up my purse and give him the money to kill himself. You did that," Vera responded loudly.

Those words rendered Therese speechless. With a wave of her hand, she indicated that she wanted Vera to leave. A short while later, she closed the door of her room, then she removed the cloth belt from her bathrobe. She pulled a chair over to the closet, stood on the chair, and tied one end of the belt around the bar that held the clothes. She made a loop out of the other end of the belt, put her head through, and tightened it. Finally, she kicked the chair out from under her, intending to hang herself.

Fortunately, the bar was of the type that collapses when too much weight is put on it. Such bars are frequently used in mental institutions to circumvent just such an action as Therese's. The bar buckled and sent Therese crashing to the ground. When the nurses found her, she wasn't severely hurt, but she was hysterical and had to be heavily sedated.

When Vera told Edie what had happened, she was terribly upset. She felt bad and about as guilty as she was capable of feeling. Yet some indignation remained. "Maybe I spoke too harshly to Therese," she confessed. "I'll admit that. She made me so angry, pestering me for more attention. What about somebody giving *me* some attention? But I didn't mean to do anything to hurt her. And no matter what Therese said, I know I've been a good mother."

Her words were tantamount to stepping inside a tiger's

cage. Edie pounced. She told Vera that she hadn't been a good mother at all. She had been a neglectful one. Had Vera ever listened to how she sounded when she talked about her children? Well, Edie had, and she had taken copious notes. She took out those notes and began to read. "He was always whining, tugging at my skirts." "She's an emotional cripple, just like her brother." "The trouble I had with him." "She's always been a burden."

Then Edie informed Vera that it wasn't only what she said, but how she said it, with contempt no caring mother would use. She made Vera repeat the words back to her until she got the tone right.

"I don't think she had ever really listened to herself before," Edie commented. "It stopped her cold."

"Put her in cold storage, you mean," I said. I speculated aloud that Vera had been too numbed by the assault to do anything but what Edie told her to do. And like a person who experiences physical trauma, Vera's real pain probably didn't begin until some time after the event. Undoubtedly, she was at home now experiencing a renewed dose of depression.

I felt myself getting hot with anger. "You really enjoyed making her suffer, didn't you?" I asked.

"Of course not," Edie countered. "I'm helping her to grow and change. If she doesn't realize what she's been doing, she can't change."

I told Edie that I wasn't buying her explanation. We had thoroughly discussed the importance of not beating up on a patient. In fact, she had agreed not to do it, and now she had mounted a major assault. I knew that Edie had been sorely pressed by Vera's lack of insight. Vera's behavior could have caused Therese's death. But that didn't justify the way Edie struck out at her. What she had done to her wasn't therapy. It was a brand of sadism, I told her.

"What an awful word," Edie sniffed, sinking back in the chair.

"It may be, but it's an accurate one," I emphasized.

Edie began to cry, and I felt quite rotten. My attack on her could have been characterized as sadism, too. I knew she was bringing out the worst in me, subconsciously getting me to treat her as she had treated others. Of course, I wasn't the end of the chain, just as she wasn't the beginning. Someone had hurt Edie quite badly to give her this need to hurt others.

Life itself had done it to some extent, I knew, by making her an orphan at such an early age. And her grandparents had neglected her. They were probably guilty of more than that, however. But how? Maybe Edie had more contact with them than she wanted to admit. Or maybe the brief times they were together were unpleasantly memorable.

I apologized to Edie for having been so harsh.

"Forget it, Wayne, I'm used to it," she whispered.

Now it was I who turned a firm gaze on Edie. I wouldn't lower my eyes until she lowered hers. "What gives? Your husband?" I asked.

"Oh, no, Tom's the sweetest person on earth," Edie said. "Just as sweet as I pretend to be. I was talking about my grandparents. They did some real numbers on me."

She thought for a moment, looking for a way to characterize what her grandparents had done. Then she asked me laughingly if I had ever read an old-fashioned girl's book called *Elsie Dinsmore.* When I said no, she explained that Elsie was the heroine of a popular series that appeared in the early 1900s. Motherless Elsie, a devout Christian, often comes into conflict with her father, a nonbeliever, who must inflict his will on her in the name of building character. In one incident, her father asks Elsie to play the piano for some company. But it's the sabbath, so Elsie refuses. Her father makes her sit at the piano for hours and hours, without any food, until Elsie keels over in a dead faint.

"My grandparents were like Mr. Dinsmore," Edie said. "If they had a spare minute for me, it was only for concentrated 'character building.' They did mean things to me, but 'for my own good,' so how could I complain?"

One of the worst incidents Edie remembered was being forced to learn to swim. Her grandparents' house was on a lake, and when Edie was six, her grandmother insisted that she jump off the dock and her grandfather would catch her. Edie refused. She was not only terrified of swimming, she was terrified of the lake itself. This was the lake where her parents had drowned in a boating accident. Edie believed that if she jumped in, she would die, too. Her parents were in the lake. They would drag her down to where they were.

Edie had explained all of this to her grandmother, who dismissed it as "nonsense." We all had to learn to be brave. And a lake was just a lake, she said, sitting placidly in her wheelchair on the shore. And when Edie still refused to jump, she ordered the live-in girl to pick her up and toss her in.

Edie hated her grandmother for being so mean. And later on, she found herself doing mean things, too, to other children. But as she grew older, "doing things" was no longer necessary. She saw that she could hurt others by saying certain things, like pointing out their faults, for example. "I feel so rotten inside sometimes, and for a few minutes after I've unloaded on somebody, it feels better. But then, it starts all over again." She buried her face in her hands.

Edie was a person in continuous pain. But she had alleviated some of the pain very neatly by becoming a therapist. As a therapist, she could be "rotten" to others without suffering any guilt that she was conscious of. She had honestly convinced herself that she was helping patients by forcing them to deal with their own inadequacies. Now the plug had been pulled on that escape hatch. She could no longer lie to herself. If she was going to continue as a therapist, she would have to change her style and learn to deal with her personal pain in another way.

The obvious way was to go back into therapy. I told Edie that I could recommend a few therapists who I thought would be good for her.

She demurred. "I just can't dig up all that garbage again, Wayne," she protested.

"What about your little girl? Doesn't she deserve to have a mother who isn't going to dump on her and force her to jump into the lake because 'it's good for her'? And you might, you know, even though you don't want to."

At that, the steel in Edie's gray eyes melted. I could see that I had tuned into a subconscious fear that must have been troubling her for some time. She took out a small notebook and wrote down the names I gave her. "I'll look into it, I really will," she promised.

Edie looked exhausted. She has probably had enough for one day, I thought, but we still had to face the major issue: what do do about Vera's treatment. Edie was clearly an inappropriate therapist for Vera or any other older person at this point. We agreed that she would have a long talk with the psychiatrist who was in charge of the treatment center and request that Vera be assigned to another therapist. He thought very highly of Edie, so it would take courage for her to give him all the facts. He was also Therese's therapist.

The next day, when Edie met with the psychiatrist, he told her that Therese might need additional shock treatment. He had also ordered that Vera not be allowed to visit her for the time being. But she might not have been able to visit in any case, since Vera herself was quite depressed. She had phoned the center and made an appointment with the psychiatrist. He suspected that he would have to assign her to another therapist, since she had firmly said she didn't want to see Edie anymore. Edie was a "witch," Vera had commented, and Edie couldn't argue that the appellation was far from wrong.

I heard from Edie occasionally after she herself entered treatment. She thought her therapy was progressing well, but of course, she had thought that the last time. She heard about Vera through the case conferences held at the treatment center. Apparently, it took considerable time for her to begin to trust her new therapist, who was also a young woman. She was not as "naturally empathetic" as Edie appeared to be, but she was a caring person, and Vera eventually came to see that.

When last I spoke with Edie, Vera had gone back to Hungary to visit her relatives. She spoke of staying there, but it seemed unlikely that she would. For all her talk of being burdened by Therese, her ties to her daughter were very strong.

Therese herself went to a home recommended by the hospital after she was discharged. It would prepare her to live on her own if her mother didn't return, or if she decided not to live with her mother. She had "come out of her shell" quite a bit, her psychiatrist said, and she no longer considered herself responsible for her brother's death.

As for Edie, I don't know what she is doing today. I hope she is a better therapist. If she is not, I hope she is not a therapist at all. Anger has a place in therapy only when it is expressed to help, not harm.

CHAPTER 10

The Dream of Finding a Good Father

Those of us who have suffered childhood trauma from enraged or passive parents often grow up with a profound emptiness, a constant ache of longing for an "ideal" parent. An adult dominated by the dream of finding a good father or mother is likely to be driven to seek in others the parent so crucially "absent" in childhood. Some twenty-five years ago, when I was in my mid-thirties and had been in practice for only a few years, I myself succumbed to the "dream of finding a good father" in my first in-depth treatment of an older male patient.

Everett Solomon was nearing his sixtieth birthday when he first consulted me. Tall and nattily dressed, with a crisp white handkerchief in the pocket of his double-breasted blue suit, he had an air of self-possession and immediately impressed me as being unflappable and in easy control of himself. Although therapists are well accustomed to patients whose surface appearance is strikingly belied by their inner problems, still I was surprised to discover that Everett was suffering from sexual impotence. He had struggled with it all his life, through two marriages and any number of additional relationships. None of his three attempts at psychotherapy had succeeded in helping him, and no medical cause of his condition had ever been found.

"When I judge myself in terms of what I've achieved in business," he said, after he told me about his problem, "I know my life has been a great success. But then I think of my two unconsummated marriages and a dozen unconsummated relationships, and I feel I've failed—totally failed! I've been told by doctors in the past that it's stupid to measure my self-worth by whether my penis goes up and stays up when I'm in bed with a woman. But tell me, Doctor, how else *am* I to judge myself?"

He stopped a moment, and I was startled to see his eyes fill with tears.

"What it amounts to," he went on, as he pulled out his handkerchief to wipe them away, "is that that judgment makes me *hate* myself!"

Listening and watching this man whose pain and humiliation were all but palpable, I felt a sudden surge of warmth toward him, a warmth that considerably softened my usual wariness of older men, men my father's age. I realized that in all the years I had spent growing up with my violent father, with his constant yelling and storming around the house, I had never seen him cry or express any sense of neediness. It had never occurred to me that a man of his age *could* be needy, could ever reach out a hand to me for help—as Everett so clearly was doing—instead of raising it against me in anger.

I didn't know what to make of what I was feeling, it was so unsettling. I wanted to luxuriate in the newfound tenderness toward my patient, only I didn't trust it. I felt confused and at odds with myself, and I knew that I would need help if I was going to try to help Everett—more help than I was receiving from the older female therapist I had worked with for so many years.

Millie, my therapist, was a very attractive woman nearly as old as my mother, but taller and thinner, with graying blond hair. Her dress was unremarkable but she smoked a great deal and said very little, conveying to me the message that I was going to do most of the work in making sense of the events of my past—or of my work with Everett. "I felt so warm toward him, so unthreatened," I said to her during one of our sessions, speaking of my emotions the day Everett had cried in my office. "I never felt that way with my father."

"Just remember that he's a patient," Millie replied, after a long silence, "and not your father."

"I know he is." But I was deflated by her remark. A deep sense of loss suddenly overtook me. At this moment in my work with Everett, what I needed was the support of someone who was willing to risk greater involvement.

After one or two more sessions with Everett, I turned to Barney for supervision. He had a reputation for being straight-forward, someone you could talk to about anything. I had heard of his work from a number of friends who had been in supervision with him and who had benefited enormously from his help. He agreed to see me. When I went to Barney's office it was almost the antithesis of Millie's, not nearly as austere, and chock-full of photographs and souvenirs from various trips he had taken. About sixty-five, Barney was tall and had a full head of graying hair that never seemed to be in place. His glasses intensified the dark brown color of his eyes, and his voice was deep and sonorous. It was immediately apparent to me that Barney perfectly matched my stereotype of a warm, loving father. I felt a sensation I can only describe as intensely comfortable, as if I were falling into a deep armchair in front of a warm fire. These were my projections onto Barney. Luck-ily for me, he was also a brilliant psychiatrist.

In our initial consultation, I mentioned to him that some-thing about Everett's problem drew me to him. The idea that his penis was limp and ineffectual made me feel safer with him than I would have felt with most men his age. I equated his inability to produce an erection with some inherent lack of aggression—an intuition, I would later learn, not far off the mark in terms of his actual difficulties. If he couldn't fuck, he couldn't fight with me, ran my thoughts. Ergo, he wouldn't be likely to be an angry, hurtful son of a bitch like my father.

Barney knew I was in treatment and knew and respected my therapist. So he didn't beat around the bush in his response. "It sounds to me, Wayne," he said, "that you're not being entirely honest with yourself about why you feel safe with Everett's problem. How about the idea that a potent man his age, or an angry one like your father, might arouse some fears of impotence in you, in addition to homosexual anxiety? Hence the actual ease you feel with him."

His comment made me feel very uncomfortable. "You don't pull any punches, do you, Barney?" I responded.

"It's not my style. I've never been one to take kindly to bullshit, either my own or anybody else's."

After another moment's deliberation, I went on. "That was a pretty good question, but not really a new one. It's something I've talked about a lot in my therapy. I'm sure the perennial picture I have of my father standing there with his fist upraised to strike me is also a screen for some buried memory or fantasy of him ready to shove his erection down my throat or up my butt. Only the image has never been connected in my mind with any erotic feeling. It's always been a function of just who had the greatest degree of power, he or I, and never one of love or sex or tenderness. Maybe that's why the warmth I felt toward Everett was so unsettling. I think I may have confused it in my mind with sexual desire. I guess that really wouldn't be hard to do, brought up as I was to believe that real men are never supposed to feel warmth or neediness toward other men. Only the thought that it might really be possible is pretty seductive, which is probably why I'm here right now asking for your supervision. Can you help me sift through all the bullshit, Barney? It would mean an awful lot to me."

"I'll try my best, Wayne," Barney answered, "but you're going to have to go back and talk about all of this with Millie as well. I wouldn't want to let our work simply become an avenue for you to split your transference feelings toward her by making me into the good guy and her into the bad one. You'll both have to keep on top of that. Anyway, let's go back to talking about Everett. Tell me some more about what he said when he came in to see you."

I felt a surge of excitement in listening to Barney. He was a man who conveyed a sense of strength and warmth at the same time. It was an unusual feeling, something I was completely unfamiliar with.

I told him that Everett had spoken of his wish to be as open and truthful as possible with me in our treatment, in contrast to his earlier attitude of hesitancy and secretiveness with his wives and his previous therapists. "I don't have any more time to waste," he said. "I'm going to be sixty in a few weeks and my father died when he was sixty. It's clear to me the only reason he didn't live longer was that he kept his feelings bottled up inside himself all his life. I've done the same thing for most of mine. So if I'm ever going to be happy, *now's* the time to change."

I was impressed by the seriousness of his intention. It showed a potential for change I would not have thought possible for a man of his age. I liked that and, even more, I liked Everett. I liked his warmth and engaging wit and the fact that he was a good sport—qualities I had also not previously associated with men of my father's generation. But ultimately I was drawn to Everett in those initial sessions because his childhood had, like mine, been overshadowed by a parent's violence.

In Everett's family, he told me, his mother was the prime source of terror. She was a virago, a woman with a viper's tongue, which she never hesitated to unleash on both his father and Everett. His father passively endured his wife's tirades for a long time—far too long it seemed to the terrified boy—until he would finally get up, lumber over to the kitchen sink, and spit contemptuously into it. His mother would quiet down immediately, interpreting her husband's action as a sign that if she didn't he would turn on her. Then one day, years later, when Everett was in his middle twenties, the vitriol of his mother's anger finally ate through the veneer of his father's passivity. His mother was just reaching the crescendo of one of her usual diatribes when his father rose from his chair. But instead of turning toward the sink, he turned toward her. His fists were clenched, ready to strike, and his face was contorted in fury as Everett had never seen it before. With an incoherent shout of rage, he took a step toward his wife and then collapsed on the kitchen floor, dead of a heart attack. Everett told me this horrendous end to his father's life further enhanced his own sense of sexual inadequacy, and he drew the crippling conclusion that aggression is not only dangerous but punishable by death. The connection between this distant tragedy and his sexual difficulties was all too obvious to me, especially the dire equation between ejaculation and his father's ineffectual spitting all those years.

In my own family, my father was the violent parent. However, his abuse seldom remained merely verbal but moved quickly to the physical, and all too often my mother had to throw herself between him and my brother and me in order to protect us from his assaults. Thus during my childhood, my mother, brother, and I lived in a continual state of dread, waiting for the next fight, the next occasion when my father's upraised fist might maim or even kill one or all of us. Every so often there would be a day of peace, when my father's tyranny mysteriously melted away and I had a glimpse of the geniality that might have been. I would blow up such halcyon moments into endless fantasies of a miraculous reconciliation with him, hopeful of finally having found the good father I so devoutly longed for. But such moments were fleeting and the fantasy never materialized in reality.

One such moment occurred when I was eight. My father woke me early one weekend morning to take me fishing with him. The day was warm and the tuna sandwiches we bought were wonderful. I caught a large number of fish and felt as happy as I could ever remember feeling. The other men on the boat good-naturedly ribbed my father about my catching more fish than he did and he said nothing. In the car on the way home, I laid my head against his shoulder. The smell of his sweat seemed warm and manly to me. In no time I was asleep, but after a short while I was awakened by his pushing me away. "I can't shift gears with you lying all over me," he said angrily.

"Please, Daddy," I said, "I'm sleepy."

"You'll go right to bed when we get home," he answered.

"But I want to show Mommy the fish first."

"I'll show her the fish after you go to bed."

I felt hurt by his words, as if he begrudged my moment of exhibiting my manliness to my mother. When I pleaded with him, he yelled at me to stop whining—and the day was ruined, as so many others before had been. He did not hit me, but he was so angry that some saliva dripped down along the corner of his mouth as he held his teeth clenched. "Please, Daddy," I said once again, but all I received in return was a look of scorn and rage.

Finally, during my adolescence, I stood up to my father and struck him back when he raised his fist to me one time too many. He had promised to lend me his car so I could drive my girlfriend, Laura, to her sweet-sixteen party. He knew how important it was to me, how much I cared about her and how much I needed to impress her. The afternoon of the party, I even put an extra coat of wax on the car in order to have it bright and shiny for the evening. As I went to get the keys from him, my mother got caught up in the excitement and gave me a great big hug and kiss and told me to have a wonderful time. That was all it took to make my father turn the damper on my enthusiasm.

"I've changed my mind," he said. "I don't want you taking the car out this evening. You're not a good-enough driver yet."

"But I am," I protested, my heart instantly racing at the injustice of his behavior.

"Don't you dare shout at me," he responded, as rage built quickly in his own voice. "Do you hear me?"

"I promised Laura I'd pick her up in the car. You can't do this to me. It's not fair."

"I can do anything I damn well please to you," he said, raising his fists menacingly toward my face.

"Like hell you can," I answered. And I jabbed first one of my fists and then the other hard into his body. One struck him in the belly, causing him to double up. The other landed just below his heart. He looked at me stunned and then dropped his hands to his sides, turned away, and went into his bedroom and locked the door.

My evening was ruined before it had started. While part of me knew intuitively that his cruelty was really meant for my mother, in response to the obvious sign of affection and preference she had shown to me, I was not able to empathize with my father's wounds at that moment, only with my own. I could not have cared less about all the rejection he had experienced in his life. I was concerned only with his rejection of me. I was shocked that he did not hit me back when I struck him. Somewhere deep inside of me, I almost wished that he had struck me back in order to undo the terrible scene. Now I, too, had rejected him. But I could not recapture the sense of pleasure I had felt earlier that day. My blows ended my pleasure. But they also effectively ended my father's reign of terror, although not his capacity to hurt me. The ultimate hurt would come when I was off at college and he abandoned his family. He eventually divorced my mother and remarried, but I rarely went to visit him. It was clear to me that I hated him in those years and often wished that he would die.

Thus, in our life experiences, Everett and I shared the feeling of having been cruelly shortchanged by our fathers and the mutual yearning for a loving man who would have supported us in our growing up rather than leaving us to grope our way toward manhood on our own. I didn't tell Everett about our common history, but it inspired in me a strong impulse to ease his suffering and to rescue him.

It was a heady experience to look across at that urbane older man and see how much he looked to me for help, to feel I had the power to supply him with the masculinity his father failed to provide. And even though Barney's words had seemed so unsettling to me, I could find no sexual resonance in any of the feelings I experienced toward Everett. It appeared to be more a matter of our being a perfect match, as if we had been made for each other. Although I wasn't totally conscious of it at that time, my underlying thought was that I would have been happy to have had Everett Solomon for my father instead of my real one. And, even further from consciousness, I reasoned that if I could only undo the horrors of his past, perhaps he would perform the same function for me in respect to mine. Thus we could rescue each other.

Under ordinary circumstances, my old longing for an ideal father would probably not have surfaced to the extent that it did at this time. But it can happen that in even the most ostensibly thorough of analyses, as mine had appeared to be up to that point, an important aspect of one's psyche may not be dealt with adequately until it is catalyzed by some real-life event. In the case of Everett and my response to him, that event was the fact that when he first consulted me my father had just entered the last stage of his long-standing cardiovascular disease. His imminent death reactivated all the old longings of my childhood with an intensity which I had never consciously experienced as an adult.

In this context, I realized that Barney had been correct in his assessment of why I had sought him out for supervision. It was an acting out of my angry feelings toward Millie. As I had done with my mother before her, I blamed my therapist for never having provided me with the ideal father I had always longed for. If my real father was such of a son of a bitch, then why hadn't my mother left him for someone better? And why hadn't Millie had the common sense to suggest that I get in touch with a supervisor like Barney even sooner? Why was everything always being left up to me to take care of? Why did I always have to be responsible for calling all the shots myself when I was growing up? If the interpretation was made later that I was searching for a good father in order to make me feel like more of a man, I didn't hear it. It was much easier for me then to place the blame on the external deficiencies of other people rather than on any internal deficiencies within myself.

In the early part of Everett's treatment, I basked in the warm glow of his admiration to the extent that Barney would allow. Mingled in with my patient's free associations about the daily events of his life were occasional comments about movies he had enjoyed. In one of the films he spoke of, a young gunfighter helped an aging sheriff ride a band of desperadoes out of town and restored the older man to his rightful position of authority. Everett remarked that the actor who played the gunfighter looked a lot like me.

"You know," he went on, "it's what I wanted to do with my own father—make him into a man so that he could stand up to my mother. If he'd been a man, it would have been so much easier for me to be one, too. I'd have had his tacit permission. That's one of the most important things you give me here, Doc, the permission to be a man."

I came to rely heavily on moments like that for my overall sense of well-being. "It makes me feel good to know I'm helping Everett," I told Barney.

"It looks that way," he answered. "But it's hard to tell if his mood is elevated because he has incorporated some of your enthusiasm, a sort of "transference cure," or if something more substantive is going on. What bothers me, Wayne, is how important it seems to you that he do well, as if too much of your own self-esteem is riding on his becoming a potent man. I think you ought to talk about that with Millie. It's a hell of a strain on the treatment."

Some time later, Everett mentioned that ever since the day he first came to my office he had felt we looked a lot alike. "It's uncanny," he said. "We could be father and son."

I was deeply moved by this remark, but asked what it meant to him. "If you were really my son," he replied, "it would mean that I had been a successful man in my life and a potent one."

And if you were my father, I thought to myself, you sure as hell wouldn't be an angry one like my real father.

In allowing Everett to feel I was the good son he had never had, I thought I was helping him to overcome the myriad slights to his self-esteem and the depressing image of himself as less than adequate, which had haunted him all his adult life whenever his penis failed to become or stay erect when he was in bed with a woman. And by being the good father I had never had, Everett was helping me to realize my lifelong fantasy of closeness with an older man who was loving and nurturing instead of hateful and rejecting. The immense reservoir of rage which I had felt all my life toward my father seemed to be diminishing in its intensity, and I was elated. When I spoke of these thoughts and feelings to Millie and to Barney, I felt as if I was riding on the crest of a wave. It was a high that I had no desire to climb down from.

At this point, my father died. And compounding the deeply mixed feelings that threatened to overwhelm me in the weeks and months after his death was the further shock inflicted by the terms of his will. He left his entire estate to his second wife and nothing at all to my brother and me. It was as if we, his sons, did not count in his life and somehow did not deserve to count in our own as well. I both hated my father's guts and felt totally rejected. With Everett, and to a lesser extent with Barney, I was able to feel better about myself. Only they could ease my pain. With Millie, I felt only anger. Once more, I perceived her as a mother who had failed to provide me with a good father. Even though I knew my ideas about my mother were unrealistic, I felt unforgiving. Damn her, I thought, why wasn't she ever there to protect me when I needed her? So once again I turned to Everett to love and rescue me and to be the good father I more than ever longed for.

I didn't begin to realize the depth of my feelings toward Everett until I caught myself thinking of him one day when he was away on a business trip. When I spoke of this during my own analytic hour, I began to cry. I realized I was actively missing him, his presence, an older man who allowed me to feel strong and *good for something*. After I mentioned this to Barney, he asked me when the feelings were most intense, and I said that they were most acute at the time of Everett's regular analytic sessions. The shock of recognition again brought tears to my eyes. I tried to pass them off by saying that I had not previously realized just how accurate a time-piece the unconscious was, but Barney wouldn't let me get away with that feeble attempt at deception.

"Wayne, I know this is a difficult time for you," he said, "but you've got to get a better fix on what's going on. You're walking around like a bundle of need waiting to be gratified and that's not fair to your patients or to yourself. Everett came to you so that you could grant the gift of masculinity to him, and you've come to me for the same thing. What you both don't seem to realize is that what you're looking for is within yourselves to find and not within the power of someone else outside of you to grant."

While I heard the sound of Barney's words, the resonance that accompanied them and gave them depth and meaning seemed lost on me. I just wanted to be given something warm and loving by an older man, something freely offered. I didn't want to be told that the power to give that gift lay within myself. I had spent my whole life taking care of myself, in charge of my own gift-giving. I wanted a little respite from that responsibility now.

I thought of when I had graduated from medical school and everyone in the family had come to the ceremony except my father. When I asked him about it later, he simply shrugged his shoulders and said: "I didn't want to be around your mother."

"I can understand that," I answered. "But what about me? It would have meant a lot."

"You're on your own now, Wayne. You don't need me any-more."

I just looked at him then. He must have seen the pain in my eyes because he quickly turned his own away. There was nothing more to say. There had never been very much to say between us. I never again expected him to do anything for me, yet I was crushed by his death and his final rejection of me in his will.

With Everett there was still some hope for acceptance, or

so I thought at the time. Although carrying strong feelings about a patient with you after a session is a clear-cut sign of a problem, I was soon given even more incontrovertible evidence of the intensity of my countertransference disturbance concerning Everett. It took the form of a series of dreams about him. In the first one, the cartoon character Popeye and I were strolling about the teeming streets of some Asian city. The usually unflappable sailor man seemed anxious about being in this strange place where he couldn't read the Oriental characters of the shop signs. I felt no apprehension, however; it seemed to me that I was on familiar ground. Then it struck me that I was back in Korea and I indeed recognized some of the people I knew during my military service there. As I walked toward one to say hello, I heard gunfire and people fell to the ground to avoid being hit. Hordes of soldiers appeared and began to fire at the prostrate civilians. The scene made me very angry, and fearing for Popeye's life I knew I had to get him out of harm's way. Suddenly I saw some red hot peppers drying in the sun and ate a few. A wave of strength coursed through my body and I no longer worried about the bullets from the soldiers' guns. With a flick of my wrists, I picked Popeye up—he now looked strikingly like Everett—and bore him to safety. I sighed with relief and woke up.

I understood at once that Popeye was a stand-in for my father—not only because of the word "pop" in his name but because of a memory that went back to a day in my childhood when my father, in one of his rare good moods, was showing Popeye movies on our home projector. The conflation of Popeye with Everett in the dream served to drive home the point that he was operating in my imagination as some sort of acceptable representation of my father.

While I spent a number of hours with Millie associating about the different elements in the dream, perhaps the most disturbing facet of it for me was my identification with my father. I, too, became strong and impervious to harm, by eating the hot peppers. It was difficult for me to deny to myself that the content of the dream had a homosexual flavor to it. I was ingesting my father's fiery strength by swallowing the Oriental equivalent of his hot paternal seed. And yet the feeling of the dream seemed anything but homoerotic to me. Millie suggested that I might once more be stuck on an idea I had ruminated about much of my life, that I equated my father's outbursts of violence with an inchoate attempt on his part to exhibit a distorted posture of masculinity to my mother, brother, and me. While her interpretation seemed correct to me, I was unable to use it at that moment to expand appreciably my understanding of the multiple levels of identification present within the dream.

At my next supervisory session, when I repeated the dream and the ensuing associations and interpretations to Barney, he asked: "Are you saying that you think your father was impotent, too?"

His use of the word "impotent" stunned me, and I was momentarily unable to respond. "I don't think he actually was," I finally answered. "But he must have felt locked out by my mother, brother, and me, and that couldn't have done a lot for his image of himself as a man."

"Maybe part of the warmth you feel in helping Everett," Barney said, "is related to a rescue wish toward your father that you had as a child, to help him feel more acceptable as a man."

"I don't think so, Barney. It doesn't sound right," I said, totally resisting Barney's suggestion, although something deep down inside of me recognized the correctness of his interpretation. "He never wanted to do anything for me, and I never wanted to do anything for him. Quid pro quo." I left the session feeling irritated, although I did not realize it at the time.

In the weeks and months that followed, I became increasingly aware of moments of anger toward Everett, particularly his repeated inadequacies in business dealings with more aggressive men. He was fine when dealing with matters involving tactful negotiations, but slugging it out toe-to-toe with other men wasn't exactly his forte. That aspect of him disappointed me, as if he was not living up to my expectations. In my analysis, I realized that my father had also behaved like this in his business dealings with other men, while playing the tyrant at home, and Barney's comment about my perception of him as being impotent began to take on added meaning for me.

Several months after the Popeye dream, I dreamed again about Everett. In this one, I was balancing a book on my head and, at the same time, trying to walk a straight line. The paired acts seemed impossible to perform, and the book kept falling off my head onto the floor. Finally, concentrating all of my mind on the task, I began to succeed in navigating the prescribed course. Then, as I neared the finish line, the book dropped to the floor again and opened to a page showing a relief map of the Himalayas, with Mount Everest prominently displayed. I realized that the book was an atlas and awoke feeling angry.

In thinking about the dream, I associated Mount Everest with my patient's name, Everett. I recognized that the anger that was the aftermath of the dream was connected with the sense of frustration I had recently been experiencing in Everett's treatment. That was depicted in the dream as my inability to balance the book on my head and simultaneously walk the straight line. But I had no clue as to the meaning of the atlas until about a week later when I was walking down Fifth Avenue toward Rockefeller Center. As I passed 51st Street and the looming statue there of the titan Atlas carrying the globe of the world on his shoulders, something clicked in my mind. I recognized that in the dream I had grandiosely seen myself as Atlas, attempting to carry on my own shoulders all of the burden of curing Everett's personal and sexual problems. A flimsy attempt to deny his impotence was apparent in the play on words present in the dream between Everett and Everest, the highest, most phallic-appearing mountain peak in the world. But the anger I had experienced on awakening from the dream seemed clearly to be related to my feeling that my patient was not pulling his fair share of the load in the analysis. Irritation at him again swept over me.

My annoyance with Everett increased over the next few weeks, despite the repeated attempts of Millie and Barney to help me ferret out the underlying reasons for it. Whatever I learned seemed to vanish from my awareness the moment I left my analytic or supervisory sessions. What remained with me was the curdling of my once positive feelings for my patient by my perception of him as a man as essentially unfulfilling and frustrating as my father. I had shed the fantasy of him as the "good" father, and I came to look on him in an increasingly angry way. That did not change until one morning, after a tortured night of tossing and turning, I awoke feeling an acute physical sensation of aching for my father, something I had never consciously experienced before. The anger I had felt toward him throughout most of my life seemed to dissolve a bit, replaced by sorrow.

That morning ushered in a period of real mourning for my father. I was able to examine with Millie my interactions over the years with him, to look at them one small piece at a time, and to recognize how hard it must have been for him to have had to face the unremitting hostility and fear of my mother, my brother, and myself. I thought of all the pain and terror he had caused me, and all the myriad disappointments and broken dreams. Ever so slowly over the next many months I began to put them and him to rest as best I could. In my self-scrutiny, I never went so far as to like or care for him—that was too much to ask. But I think I was finally able to accept him as a tormented human being, as I had never expected to be able to do.

Bit by bit, as I managed to forgive my father, my relations with most of my patients were subtly modified. "It's strange, Barney," I said to him one day, "how freed up I feel with most of my patients now. As if I suddenly realized that I'm the one helping them and not vice versa. It sounds ridiculous to say that, but I see it more clearly now."

"It's a basic tenet of therapy, Wayne," Barney said. "Your patients are in treatment because they hurt, not because you do. The battle to keep your needs and expectations separate from theirs is never over, never won. It can erupt when you least expect it. You have to keep on working through your own feelings over and over again."

Throughout this prolonged period of mourning for my father that lasted the better part of the second and third years of Everett's treatment, I found it harder to work with him than with any of my other patients. Even though I was aware that I was still responding to him as if he should make up to me for all the warmth and love my father had never given me, I resented his failure to do so. My lifelong resentments and disappointments were never very far from the surface, and I was aware of protecting myself from painful feelings of rage and hurt by becoming emotionally distant from Everett, or by momentary lapses of attention after which I had no recollection of what he had been saying. When I met with Barney, I attempted to revert to a technique I had not used with any of my supervisors for many years, the method of reading aloud detailed summaries of Everett's hours from the notes I had taken after each of our sessions. Finally Barney interrupted me. "Are you aware, Wayne," he asked, "that in gazing down at your notes and in obsessively detailing everything that's happened during the week that way, you're putting yourself at an enormous emotional distance from me?"

"Now that you mention it, I guess I am," I replied in a somewhat detached tone.

"And isn't that what you've been talking about in your work with Everett?"

"Yes." I nodded in agreement.

"What do you think is going on, Wayne?"

"I don't know."

"Don't you think you're trying to distance me to protect me from your anger? Not only hasn't Everett made up for all the love you never got from your father, but neither have I. A little anger isn't going to kill me, Wayne. Or even a lot. So let's go back to your talking to me without notes from now on. Okay?"

"Okay," I said, and the next few supervisory hours felt interminable as I struggled to break through the layers of insulation I had woven about me.

Then one night I had a dream in which I saw Everett stretched out on the black couch in my office. I was uncertain whether he was dead or alive and whether the couch was really a couch or a coffin. In the dream, I wanted to reach out to him and touch his face, only a translucent sheet of something like glass seemed to be separating us, making it impossible for me to get any closer to him.

"I have the feeling that Everett represents my father," I said, when I spoke of the dream to Millie. "I want to get closer, only there's a sheet of glass separating us."

"Any thoughts about the glass?" Millie asked.

"It's a protection, I think, from my getting hurt the way I did every time I tried to get close to him."

"Anything else about the glass?"

"You certainly are pushing the glass," I said, irritated. And then the sense of vexation I felt gave me a clue as to another meaning of the dream. "It protects me or them from the anger I feel."

"Them?"

"All of them. My father, Everett, Barney—I'm angry at all of them these days. No matter how much I try to get them to love me, I come up empty-handed. I want to lash out and scream at them, to destroy them. No wonder I've distanced myself in my sessions with Barney lately. He's already called me on it. It's what I did with my father ever since I was a little boy."

"I know he was the only model that you had," Millie answered, "but you don't become a man by yelling louder than anyone else or lashing out at the world the way your father did. It's something that you feel inside of you, that you know is there. Something that neither Barney nor I nor anyone else can give to you."

I hated what Millie was saying, but I knew she was right. Unfortunately, old wishes take a long time to die. And the wish for a good father to make me feel like a man was a very old wish of mine.

Barney lit up when I came in the next week and presented the dream to him, just as he had previously been excited when I mentioned my earlier dreams about Everett. "You know, Wayne, there's practically nothing in the analytic literature about using your dreams as a means of monitoring counter-transference feelings. I've often thought of writing something about it, but with all this stuff about Everett, I think that you should be the one to do it. Take another look at Freud's dream about Irma in *The Interpretation of Dreams* and you'll have some second thoughts about his understanding of it. He obviously felt humiliated by Irma in front of his colleagues, and the dream clearly expressed his wishes to get even with her for 'doing that' to him."

I realized that what Barney was doing for me then was trying to pique my intellectual curiosity and at the same time diminish my feelings of guilt about my handling of Everett's case. It was only later that I came to understand that his suggestion was also his way of giving me permission to be in competition with him as a man and as an analyst. That's the way it is with great supervisors. Sometimes you don't even realize when you're being most profoundly affected by them. It may take years before the recognition finally sinks in, as it took me years before I ultimately wrote that article.

As the months went on, I began to feel easier in my interactions with Everett. I realized that my needs in our relationship had ceased to be neurotic ones. The change, which had been imperceptible at first, soon stood out in bold relief as I finally began to accept the flawed human being behind my father's rageful outbursts. Barney's words about that kind of emotional bondage still ring clearly in my mind today: "Nothing is ever truly in the past, Wayne, as long as it still operates in the present." And in finally understanding and coming to terms with the reasons for my father's tirades in the past, I was able to pry him loose from the present tense of my life. As best as I could comprehend, he had always been rejected throughout his life, first as an unwanted child within his family and then when both of his parents had died when he was very young. When he realized that my mother never really loved him, it simply intensified his lifelong feelings of being unlovable, and he grew more and more embittered with her and with us, more and more angry. And finally, in the classic style of the abandoned, rejected child, he became a viciously rejecting, abandoning parent. When I came to view him in that light, he was no longer alive for me in the old way. My work with Barney and with Millie finally allowed me to be able to bury him once and for all, if "once and for all" can ever be the case.

When my renewed good feelings for Everett began to be something that Barney and I could take for granted, he raised the possibility that we should soon stop our supervision, and I agreed. Not that I had nothing more to learn from him. But we both realized that to continue the supervision would have been a way of reinforcing the unhealthy perception of myself as being less than an adequate man, someone in the mold of my father, an image that was now an anachronism. It was as important for me to dispel that image within myself as it was for Everett to do so within himself.

Some time after I stopped the supervision with Barney, I had another dream about Everett. In it, he and I were decked out in track suits preparing to perform at a meet, at a javelin throw. As the judge called out the opening commands, we both raised our arms high and then hurled the javelins far off into the distance. After completing our initial throw, we each in turn fired off a second salvo and then looked over at an older man sitting in the grandstand. He raised his hat in salute to us, and we both smiled back at him.

When I associated to the dream afterward, it seemed satisfyingly clear. The ease with which both Everett and I had handled the phallic javelins confirmed the perception that we were both more confident about ourselves as men. The initial simultaneous salvo referred to the old fantasy that to be adequate men we needed each other or a strong father to aid us. The second individual throws reflected the fact that in reality we were both more than adequate in our own right. Neither of us needed to rescue the other anymore. The older man in the grandstand, saluting our masculine prowess, was either Barney or some newly benign version of our respective fathers. All in all, I thought, a remarkably positive dream.

Just at this time, Everett's analysis really began to take off. In fact, I came to believe that my dream was a preconscious recognition of the positive processes that had been taking place within my patient's psyche for some time. He was soon painstakingly working through his feelings about his father. And slowly but surely over the six years of his analysis, he severed the unhealthy connections between aggression and dire punishment that had troubled him for so many decades. In so doing, he thoroughly repudiated Freud's dire predictions about older people being unable to be helped by psychoanalysis. Before concluding his treatment with me, he formed a new and better relationship with a woman than any he had had before, attained the sexual potency that had eluded him all his life, and married—this time very happily—for the third time.

His death some years later brought a brief recurrence of the painful feelings I had experienced after my father's death and of the fantasy that had disturbed Everett's treatment. Once again, although with considerably more ease this time around, I had to lay to rest the dream of finding a good father. And while I still did not ever come to like my father, my ancient hatred seemed considerably muted. When a mother or a father has cruelly tyrannized one's childhood, a tentative acceptance of that parent may be all the adult can ever reasonably hope for. If total acceptance and love aren't quite possible to attain, it's at least a way of finally letting go of them.

Many years later, I was saddened to hear of Millie's death. The years we spent together were important ones for me and added many new and valuable insights to my life. Through her silence, she allowed me to find my own strength and to mitigate my anger toward my father. My expectations about her giving me a better father became muted as I slowly began to forgive my mother for not having had the courage it would have taken to leave my father when my brother and I were children. As I came to accept my mother's limitations, I accepted as well the limitations life imposes on all of us. And in this acceptance, I found the strength to be a better father myself when the time came than my own father had been. For that, I would always be grateful to Millie. She was not a warm woman but she was a strong one and her strength blessed my life.

The announcement in the newspaper of Barney's death evoked another kind of pain and gratitude. Although we had not spent as much time together as I had spent with Millie, I perceived his effect on me as being one of the most positive experiences of my life. He helped to rescue me from a countertransference morass that threatened to disrupt my early years as a therapist. More than anyone else, he taught me to value the dreams that emerge in my life and work as a psychotherapist—both the ones that transfigure my own and my patients' sleep at night, and the ones that fuel my attitudes toward my patients during the day. Freud referred to night dreams as the royal road to the understanding of the unconscious minds of our patients. With Barney's help, I learned that the dreams we have at night are also a royal road to understanding our own countertransference feelings toward our patients.

Many years have passed since my encounters with Everett and Barney. Today, I'm the same age as Everett was when he first began his treatment with me. When I think of him and of Barney, I still have occasional pangs of nostalgia for the father I so obviously lacked and longed for. But I am confident that I have at least internalized the best of Barney's teachings, and know that my own shrink dreams will no longer get the best of me again. In that sense, Barney's positive influence, like that of all good fathers with their children, will be with me for the rest of my life.

AFTERWORD

After you have read some of the abuses that may occur in the name of therapy, you may wonder how to avoid being subjected to such excesses when seeking help. While I have no perfect answer to that question, I have some thoughts to offer which I hope will be of value.

In the initial session, if you have questions about your prospective therapist's training, by all means ask them then, rather than waiting for some later date to be surprised or disappointed with the answers. One of the perfectly reasonable lines of inquiry to pursue deals with the subject of whether the therapist has had therapy of his or her own. While the wish to know something about the therapist may very well be derived from unconscious problems you will work out in therapy, it is a reasonable and even important request. As such, it merits being dealt with in a respectful and straightforward manner by the therapist. It is important to know that the person in whose hands you place your trust is well trained and has had therapy to deal with any blind spots. While this may not be an absolute guarantee that you will avoid the potential pitfalls of countertransference, it is at least a start.

Once you have entered into a psychotherapeutic treatment, how can you tell if the therapist is experiencing strong countertransference feelings that may impede your treatment? While again there is no easy answer to that question, here are some guidelines to help you decide when a treatment is going awry.

It is of primary importance that any patient feel the therapist is a caring, respectful, and understanding person. I hesitate to add that you should also feel that the therapist likes you, even though this is a given in most successful treatments. Patients who have felt unlovable in their lives are going to bring this feeling with them into treatment, and may need a little more time to make a reasonable evaluation.

What is more important to be on guard against in terms of countertransference feelings is the perception that the therapist feels too strongly about you, in either the positive or negative sense. Unless these feelings are clearly a projection of your own long-standing problems with other people, perceptions such as these in the therapeutic situation are clear-cut danger signals of an overheated countertransference. I would caution most patients to err on the side of trusting their own feelings, and to confront the therapist with their doubts as they arise.

Some signs of a negative countertransference are when the therapist often seems irritable, or frequently forgets details of what you have told him, or seems bored, detached, or sleepy, or is overly critical and given to making peremptory judgments about your actions. While good therapy may often entail a painful probing of the past and the present, intrusive questions which seem primarily geared to meeting the therapist's needs rather than your own are another hint that something may be wrong. Inordinately positive responses to you may result in a failure on the therapist's part to ask probing questions, because he feels they may be "too painful" for you. And obviously, if the therapist begins to make sexually provocative or inappropriate suggestions or advances, beat as hasty a retreat as possible from the treatment.

If you have questions about your therapist's being in the throes of a countertransference bind, bring this up in the treatment and do not let your questions go unanswered. If your queries at such a time are met only with questions in return, be very wary about continuing with the therapist. If you have strong doubts, suggest the idea of a consultation with an experienced psychotherapist to evaluate the nature of the difficulties in your treatment and to suggest what paths to take to obviate them. If the therapist balks at this suggestion after a reasonable discussion, you are probably better off leaving such a treatment. Blind defensiveness on the part of the therapist is not in your best interests.

One final question seems worth mentioning here. Should a patient know that his or her therapist is in supervision? In most of the psychoanalytic centers in our country, the application forms sent to prospective patients indicate that the candidates in training as therapists on their staffs are being supervised in their treatments. Most people in the field, such as psychiatrists, psychologists, social workers, nurses, and physicians automatically assume that younger people in training are being supervised. In a survey I conducted on this issue at the Columbia University Center for Psychoanalytic Training and Research, patients seemed to view supervision as a plus in their treatment, protecting them against abuses by their therapists. Similar reports have been found in other training sites.

Older, presumably more experienced therapists should theoretically be less likely to be swayed by unresolved countertransference factors. Unfortunately, this is not always the case, inasmuch as all therapists can be afflicted by countertransferences beyond their control, depending on the balance of emotional forces in their own lives at any given time. Only ongoing monitoring of the therapist's unconscious, or an occasional return for further therapy, can prevent this difficulty. A perceptive patient may often tune into the idea of some sort of change in the therapist's technique after the therapist enters supervision. I do not necessarily believe that therapists have to inform their patients when they enter supervision, but I would certainly not recommend that they deny it if a patient

AFTERWORD

asks. It is hardly a sign of weakness or inadequacy for a therapist to recognize the need for help in dealing with countertransference feelings. To acknowledge this to a patient is more a sign of the therapist's caring than an admission of weakness.

An observation I made much earlier in this book bears repeating. Any successful treatment is a collaboration between therapist and patient—and honesty is the rule we must all respect.

ACKNOWLEDGMENTS

To begin with, I want to acknowledge the aid of two very special people whose unstinting support helped me bring this book to fruition. The first is Phoebe Hoss, who was one of the individuals instrumental in getting me to begin work on the book. Her calming presence and sage counsel helped me get through the early parts of this work. The second is Jean Arbeiter, whose upbeat manner and seminal suggestions concerning the final sections of this book were also of inestimable value. I warmly salute them both.

For my agents and friends, Nancy and Herb Katz, I reserve my warmest feelings and my admiration. They have helped nurture this project for a very long time. It would never have seen the light of day without them. I cannot thank them enough for all their time, their caring, and their infinite attention to detail.

Fred Hills, my editor at Simon & Schuster, is another of the special people connected with this book. His faith, trust, and editorial acumen, along with the good work of his colleague Burton Beals, gave me the direction that resulted in the manuscript's final shape.

My wife, Joanne, has always been there for me as a bulwark of strength, in addition to being my literary muse and the inspiration of my life. My children, Tracy and Blake, have also

ACKNOWLEDGMENTS

been endlessly supportive of my endeavors, and I dearly love them both.

I would be remiss if I were to omit thanking my former supervisors, my analyst, my supervisees, and my patients, who have taught me most of what I know about the practice of psychotherapy.

Finally, no list of acknowledgments would be complete without mention of the extraordinary secretarial and administrative help offered to me by Martha Garvey, Lutricia Perry, and Joan Jackson. Thanks again to all of you.

About the Author

Wayne Myers, M.D., is Clinical Professor of Psychiatry at
Cornell University Medical Center's Payne Whitney Clinic,
and Attending Psychiatrist at New York Hospital. He is also
a training and supervising psychoanalyst at the Columbiá
University Center for Psychoanalytic Training and Research.
The author of several books on psychiatry and psychoanalysis, he lives in New York City.